The Family Guide to
TRAINING YOUR DOG

D1361792

The Family Guide to
TRAINING YOUR DOG

Björn Olson   Photography by Ulla Sundén

Sterling Publishing Co., Inc. New York

**Library of Congress Cataloging-in-Publication
Data Available**

This book has been edited, designed, and produced by
Johnston Editions, Sweden.

Text: Björn Olson
Photography and design: Ulla Sundén
Advisory board: Jan-Erik Karlsson,
Elisabet Hellgren, Anita Norrblom

10 9 8 7 6 5 4 3 2 1

Published in 1991 by Sterling Publishing Company, Inc.
387 Park Avenue South, New York, N.Y. 10016
Originally published in Sweden by Rabén and Sjögren
under the title *Hunden: Val Träning Vård*
© 1991 by Streiffert & Company
Distributed in Canada by Sterling Publishing
c/o Canadian Manda Group, P.O. Box 920, Station U
Toronto, Ontario, Canada M8Z 5P9.
Distributed in Australia by Capricorn Ltd.
P.O. Box 665, Lane Cove, NSW 2066.
Printed and bound in Italy.
All rights reserved.

Sterling ISBN 0-8069-8497-X

CONTENTS

FOREWORD

The fact that you have bought a dog does not automatically mean that it will be your devoted and faithful friend for the rest of its life. A dog's love cannot be bought for money, it can only be won if you succeed in creating a positive relationship based on mutual respect, understanding, and trust. To be a good dog owner, you must learn to know your dog – and yourself, keeping in mind that it is not just a dog that you acquire, it is another wolf in your pack. If you realise this and act accordingly, you will come to experience that special love that only a dog can give – unselfish, unlimited and unconditional. It is a love worth reciprocating, not just when your dog is a lovable little puppy or a handsome animal in its prime, but also when age dulls its eye and slows its movements. When you allow a dog into your life, you are getting a lifetime companion.

This book is dedicated to Kim

CHOICE
AND
UPBRINGING

WHICH BREED?

This is a question that all prospective dog owners should ask before getting a dog. Far too many dogs are bought on impulse. 'Please, may I have a dog! *Everybody* else has one! One of those cute ones that my best friend has...' It is hard to resist that line of argument – and then the choice has been made. Or one is lured by an advertisement which says 'Super sweet cross-bred puppies. Bargain price to good home'. Unfortunately, the low price is also a factor that too often plays a decisive role in choosing a dog. But a dog is not an everyday purchase that can be returned or changed if it does not suit its owner. So think before you choose.

There are over four hundred dog breeds in the world. If you add the innumerable amount of mixed breeds – with ever new combinations – you will see that the choice is not very easy. Each breed has its own characteristics, which have been inherited through many generations and which have sometimes been deliberately strengthened by breeding.

These cannot be altered easily, just as your own deeply rooted habits are not very easy to change either. To make matters even more complicated, individual dogs of the same breed often have different qualities.

To a certain extent you and your dog will adapt to each other as time goes by. But remember that what you are getting is a companion to share its life with you, so you must be careful to choose the right dog from the start. The dog has no choice – and bear in mind that if it had, it might not choose you! You must accept it on its own terms. That is why you must get to know both yourself and the breed you are thinking of buying before you sign a purchase contract.

There are a number of questions to ask yourself before you make up your mind. We can start with two simple ones. Whether you buy a dog or not might depend on your answers.

Have you and your family been tested for allergies? The result might make you forget

10

all about buying a dog, close this book, try to hand it back to your bookshop and buy a gold fish for the money. Changing dogs does not help.

Do any of your close relatives or friends suffer from dog phobia? Then the first choice is not primarily between dog breeds but between relatives and friends on the one hand and any dog at all on the other.

What else can you ask yourself? (Yes, it is true that some of these questions will make you consider whether you should get a dog at all. It is certainly not the author's intention to deter you. On the contrary. These questions – and they are far from all that should be asked – just show the importance of getting to know yourself as a dog owner so that you can choose the right dog for yourself and for which you are the right owner.)

The first question is: 'What do you want the dog for?' For company (eg, a poodle),

Sometimes, the size of your car must dictate your choice of breed . . .

for hunting (eg, a springer spaniel or a pointer) or as a guard dog (eg, an alsatian)?

If you want a companion, do you then want an easily trained family dog like a collie, or a nice and happy boxer, which everybody can like and get along with, or a typical one-person dog like a dobermann? In the latter case you will have to take into account that the whole, or the greatest part, of the responsibility for bringing up the dog and looking after it, will be yours.

Would you like an energetic, active dog like a bearded collie or an even-tempered one that takes life a bit easier, like an English bulldog? Are you yourself energetic and active, or do you like to take life easy? How much time can you set aside for your dog? A strong, lively dog like a rottweiler needs several hours of exercise daily, but do not believe that a small dog like a Yorkshire terrier needs less exercise just because it has shorter legs. If you are not very energetic, it would be better to choose an easy-going bulldog instead.

Do you work all day and do you have to leave your dog on its own? Then, frankly, the best thing might be not to get a dog at all. It is not good for a dog to be alone for a whole working day. The dog is a gregarious animal, even if some dogs cope better with solitude than others. So, you must gradually get it accustomed to being on its own, and that takes time.

What are your living quarters like? You and a great dane would hardly fit into a small one-room apartment. Having a dog in town demands certain requirements both of the dog and its owner. Do you have far to go to exercise your dog, for instance? Or must it be kept on the lead because of traffic?

The dog is a kind of wolf and there is no typical town dog. But with good training and attentive owners, many companion dogs can cope very well with life in a town. If you live in a house with a garden or have a house in the country you have a greater range of breeds from which to choose, and the environment in which you live is better for all breeds of dog (and maybe for you, too).

What is your family like? A dog is the responsibility of the whole family and that, of necessity, makes the choice a compromise. If everybody agrees to look after the dog, it might also mean being able to choose from a wider range.

How much money are you prepared to invest in your dog? Talk to friends who have dogs and find out how much it costs to give a normal sized dog a healthy, well-balanced diet. On top of that comes accessories like leads, food bowls, basket and toys (or chewed slippers if you are not careful!). Travelling on public transport also costs money, as do vaccinations, visits to the vet, boarding kennels, trimming and other care (how much do you want to learn to do yourself?), and, if you are interested, shows. These are just a few of the expenses. It is almost like having another child in the family, but without receiving Child Benefit.

What are your habits in other respects? Do you travel much – on holidays, for instance – and, if so, could your dog go with you? Or do you have somebody who will look after your dog?

How permanent is your home? Does your job make you move often? Dogs still think in terms of territory and a frequent change of environment is not good for them.

If you are looking for a hunting dog, some questions are obvious and some are the same as those that apply to a companion dog. How much do you hunt? How often, and what? What kind of life can you offer your dog when you are not hunting?

If you are looking for a guard dog, it is even more important to answer the questions honestly. Do you only want it to bark as a warning? Or should it also be able to defend you, or even to attack if necessary? Education, training and looking after hunting dogs and guard dogs demand so much of the owner that the matter is outside the scope of this book. If you are interested, a great deal of detailed specialist literature is available.

If your furniture is a light velour, don't choose a hairy dog!

WHERE SHALL I BUY MY DOG?

The daily newspapers often contain columns of advertisements where not only 'wonderful', 'cute', 'sweet' but also 'inexpensive' puppies are offered to interested buyers. Even if this is the kind of dog you would like to have, the truth is that dogs sold in this way rarely correspond to the description. Often these advertisements are for mongrels – 'accidents' – on which the seller hopes to make some money. All are sold according to the principle, 'As we've been lumbered with them, let's try to make some money out of them.' And these puppies are often very cheap, which is, too often, a convincing sales argument. It happens, unfortunately, that prospective buyers think they can take such a puppy for a trial period. So, what if it does not turn out satisfactorily? 'The children got tired of it', 'It turned out too expensive' or 'We really didn't have time for the mutt'. And what happens then to the little puppy?

Irresponsible trading with live animals should not be allowed.

This does not imply that there is anything wrong with dogs of mixed breed. On the contrary, they often have both charm and irresistible appeal. But it frequently happens that the seller has no knowledge of the puppy's pedigree, so the buyer knows nothing about its inherited characteristics or its disposition. The sweet little puppy can develop into a huge animal weighing 100lb (45kg) or more, which nobody in the family can manage, or it can be a dog with marked instincts for hunting, or it can grow to be a fat little 'sausage' and nothing like the elegant pet dog you dreamt of. The statutory rules regarding refunds do not apply in these cases. If you buy a dog, you are responsible for it and this you have to accept, even if it does not turn out the way you thought it would.

A well-run kennels is probably the best guarantee for a good puppy

You must be careful even when dealing with pedigree dogs. The dog is a popular pet and the demand for certain breeds can sometimes be great. How many collies did the film *Lassie* sell? The demand can be so great that less scrupulous breeders go in for forced breeding and sell puppies that are undernourished, badly treated and even have serious physical and psychological defects. It has become, quite simply, a seller's market and too many puppies, which for different reasons should not have been sold, have been imposed upon gullible buyers, thus ruining the breed for a long time.

To ensure that you get the puppy you want and which really will suit you, you should turn to a responsible breeder, preferably somebody who has been recommended by other dog owners and who has had good experience of his or her animals. It does not matter if it is a kennel where they breed extensively on a commercial basis or an individual owner who breeds occasionally from a bitch. The main thing is that the recommendations are good. But you must also rely on your own judgement. Do the puppies at the kennels look well fed, happy and confident? Do they have enough space to move and are the surroundings clean and neat? What is the relationship between the owner and his or her dogs? All these factors are important and affect the character and well-being of your dog. When you go to a breeder, take somebody with you who is knowledgeable about dogs. You always have the option of turning to the Kennel Club or a similar organisation, which can recommend suitable breeders. Unfortunately, many people associate the word 'kennel' with something negative and believe that it means large packs of dogs in exercise yards, and less reputable dog dealers use the expression 'privately bred' as a sales gimmick. Most reputable kennels have a name registered with the Club, which is always given to the puppy as a first name. This serves as a guarantee of good pedigree. The Kennel Club will also help you to check the pedigree of the dog you intend to buy, and this is recommended, because pedigree documents are sometimes tampered with.

The strongest will and the hottest temperament can be found in the smallest dog

WHICH PUPPY SHOULD I CHOOSE?

First and foremost, you must decide whether you should buy a puppy at all. If you are intending to have your dog for a purpose that requires specialised training – for instance, for hunting or as a guard dog – it might be better to buy an adult dog, especially if you have little experience of training dogs.

Buying a puppy is like buying a 'pig in a poke' – you never know what kind of dog you are getting or how you will cope. But being able to follow a good puppy during the whole of its growing-up period and moulding it with patience and love into the devoted, well-adjusted and happy dog you dreamed of, is a wonderful experience.

Above all, you must decide on the sex of your puppy. Apart from the obvious physical difference, there are few great differences between a bitch and a dog, so it is mainly a matter of preference.

A bitch on heat with a protection panty

Bitches are as a rule smaller than dogs, a little 'softer' and of a somewhat calmer disposition. But the difference is not so great that it cannot be adjusted by good training.

The greatest problem with a bitch is her coming into heat. She is on heat for three weeks, twice a year, and exercising her can then be difficult, as you have to fight an uneven battle with canine suitors paying their respects with great obstinacy. Some bitches bleed quite heavily during their season and it might be necessary to put on a so-called bitch protection panty. This prevents her from staining carpets and furniture. It is not, however, a safe contraceptive. It may act as a practical obstacle to mating, however, so that you have time to interfere before anything actually occurs.

A male dog can be difficult if he comes close to a bitch on heat and he can, as a part of the sex battle, become more aggressive towards other dogs competing for favours. He will mark his territory by cocking his leg and urinating on trees, poles and house corners – and in towns in particular, where authorities do not take a kind view of fouling dogs, this can lead to trouble.

As part of guarding his territory the dog likes to stop and sniff at 'messages' from other dogs when you are out walking. In the end this becomes rather irritating, but not much can be done about it. On the other hand, it must not go too far. You might be able to distract your dog so that he gets more interested in you and what you are doing or saying.

When should you buy a dog? There are dogs for sale all year round, but the biggest choice is usually available in summer. The puppies can then run outside in the sun and get exercise and as a rule grow healthier and stronger. It is also easier to house-train a dog in summer: as the problem is to get it quickly outside when the moment comes, you do not have to put on an overcoat first. Accidents will definitely happen if you have to have time to put on your coat before you go outside!

A puppy's way of eating will say a lot about its character

Many people think that a puppy is a suitable gift for Christmas or birthdays, which almost guarantees that things will go wrong from the start. The puppy is leaving its territory, which consisted of a small area inhabited only by its dam, its siblings and the breeder. Arriving in the midst of family festivities, maybe with a bearded, 'ho-ho-ho'ing Father Christmas, heaps of rustling Christmas paper and lots of people who all want to stroke the 'cute little dog', might be a problem even for the most well-balanced puppy. Such a reception could damage it for life. Peace, harmony, love, attention and care are needed to make the puppy adapt to its new territory – and that is hardly associated with Christmas or birthday celebrations.

It is important that the puppy you finally select has the best possible pedigree. Unfortunately not even the best pedigree is a guarantee that the puppy will turn out well when it is fully grown, but the chances are definitely greater. You can check the puppy's pedigree by asking the seller to show you its family tree and then find out whether, for instance, any ancestor took part successfully in a dog show or gained merit in any other way.

The way puppies eat can give you important information about their character. If you choose the leader type – the strongest, most forward puppy, the puppy who is well ahead at the feeding bowl and helps himself at the expense of the other puppies – it could have its risks. Remember the wolf pack. You might buy the future pack leader and, when it leaves the kennels, its pack is going to consist of you and your family, so there may well

A little mite can become mighty big!

der on aggressiveness and it goes without saying that you should not buy a dog of that kind. If you want to have a certain edge to your dog, it is easier to put that edge on a quiet and well-balanced dog than it is to quieten a dog that bites and is aggressive.

Do not, on the other hand, fall for the temptation to buy the puppy that is pushed aside, just because you feel sorry for it. This easily happens when children are present at the puppy selection. Sentiments of this kind come easier to children, but you, as a parent, should not fall for arguments like this.

Why not select a somewhat gentler type? Contact with such a dog will probably come more easily, as will bringing it up to become a good "member of the pack". But do not confuse gentleness with shyness, nervousness or poor physical condition. A simple test is suddenly to clap your hands. You should not buy a puppy which jumps with fright or, even worse, runs away to hide.

If you decide to buy a pedigree dog – which will be expensive – you must, of course, see that you get a dog with as many features of the breed as possible, especially if you intend to show it at some future date or to use it for breeding. Deciding how a puppy will look when fully grown is difficult, and the best thing is to get an expert on your chosen breed to assist at the purchase. You can then get help in deciding if, for example, the puppy's colouring, markings and proportions are right, if the back is built the right

be a tough leadership contest between you. If you let the dog win you have made a bed of nails for yourself – and it is not the dog's fault.

In the worst cases, forwardness might bor-

A harmonious puppy can sleep peacefully anywhere

way, if the position of the tail and the angles of the legs are correct, and if the shape of the head, position of the ears and size of the eyes and other appearance requirements for the breed are met.

Every puppy purchase must be confirmed by a purchase agreement. Dog organisations of most countries have standard forms for this which you should use. The agreement includes your right to return the puppy in case it turns out that there is something seriously wrong with it which could not be discovered at the time of the purchase. It usually contains a clause whereby the seller has the first right to repurchase if for some reason the buyer cannot keep the dog. Reputable sellers prefer to reserve the right for themselves to place the puppy in a suitable home.

It is fitting in this context to warn against taking a 'holiday' dog. It is easy to fall for the temptation to buy a puppy in dog markets abroad or to take care of quite charming, older strays. 'He chose us. He came to our restaurant every day. He looked at us with pleading eyes. We didn't have the heart to leave him.' Do you recognise the arguments?

Firstly, it is forbidden to smuggle in dogs from abroad because of the risk of rabies. Fines are large if you are caught and the risk of this is high. Secondly, if you choose to import it legally, quarantine costs are very expensive. Furthermore, you will have no idea of the kind of dog you are getting. The fight for survival among strays is tough and those that have survived a number of years are definitely not suitable pets.

As mentioned above, buying a puppy is something of a lottery, and most new dog owners now and then become discouraged when they are training their dogs. 'Did I select the right puppy?' is often their worried question. On the whole, the question is irrelevant. Ultimately, it is up to you to decide the conditions within your pack. You are responsible for how your dog develops. It is you who forms its behaviour and it is you who will be rewarded by the unreserved love and devotion of which it is capable. And that, believe me, is worth all the trouble in the world!

"So which of us is going to be pack leader, you or me?"

WELCOME HOME

When Neil Armstrong walked on the moon, he said that his small step was a big step for mankind. It is just about as big a step for a puppy when it moves from its protected life with dam and siblings to your house. Neil Armstrong could feel safe in the belief that 'the new world' he stepped onto had the advantage of being unpopulated, but the puppy's new territory is full of strange live beings and dead objects that it has not seen before.

Just imagine the puppy's first meeting with a small child. With a happy smile and arms outstretched (either to be cuddled or to keep its balance) and eyes shining with curiosity, the toddler makes straight for the puppy. For any dog, all this signals a threat. Stiff legs, stiff movements, outstretched arms, teeth showing and eyes staring. It could not be much worse. (Except, of course, that it could have been twins!)

Do not desert the newcomer by putting it down in the middle of the floor and leaving it there. The wide floor is as big as the Sahara Desert and all kind of dangers might lurk over there under the furniture. And what happened to the safe, warm arms? If you are 6 feet tall and are towering over the few inches of puppy, then it will feel very insecure. So squat down and talk in a friendly and calm manner to the puppy when you put it down on the floor in its new home. Let it slowly and in its own good time start to discover its new territory. But it is important to establish immediately that the puppy is now part of a pack and will be given its allotted place in it. It is up to you to show from the very start who is the pack leader!

A puppy is normally unafraid and curious, and the expeditions will soon get longer. Just remember to remove such things as vases and

'Puppy-prepare' the house: forbidden things out of reach, toys on the floor

your puppy swallowing small pieces of leather and so on, you have just invited it to chew the rest of your shoes. For a dog, all shoes are similar, and if it is allowed to chew one it will think that it may chew all shoes. Even a dog is consistent!

You will need other pieces of equipment before you bring home your new family member. Among other essential items are a collar and a lead. A rolled leather collar or a chain-link is the best. Broad leather collars often have hard edges and rub against the dog's fur. The lead should be of sturdy leather, preferably with a piece of chain at the end. Many dogs like biting, pulling and tearing at the lead – a rather annoying habit which must broken – and a piece of chain does not directly invite chewing. You can also buy a 'flexi-lead' which gives the dog a lot of freedom of movement but at the same time enables you to keep it under direct control.

In this big, strange new world the puppy

Feeling safe is important to the new puppy

potted plants which stand on the floor. A small puppy possesses unsuspected powers and can overturn surprisingly large objects. Remove also any possible dangers. A 'snake's nest' of electrical wires for lamps, stereo and TV is irresistible for a playful puppy. And that kind of wire might be his last chew!

Suitable toys, preferably ox-hide chews, are available in pet shops. It is certainly fun to watch the puppy dancing around with a rubber ball but do not let it ever play with one unsupervised. With its sharp little teeth it can bite off pieces with astounding ease, pieces which can threaten its life if swallowed. Toys for dogs must be chosen with as much care as toys for children.

For some reason, dogs seem to be particularly fond of playing with old, well-used shoes. You might then think that it is a good idea to give the new puppy an old slipper to chew, tear and shake. (Shaking is inherited from the wolf – it was a way of breaking the neck of the prey.) But, apart from the risk of

needs a secure place which you must have prepared in advance. In the beginning you can make do with a sufficiently large cardboard box in which you have put a cushion or a blanket. If you prefer to buy a special dog bed, take care that you get one which is stable and not too big – a little puppy can feel very lonely in his own bed, too. You can buy a bigger one later when the puppy has grown. A bed is also easier to clean than a basket. Surprising amounts of gravel and dirt stick to four puppy paws and just as you do not want crumbs in your bed, so the puppy does not want gravel and rubbish in his.

A basket also has the disadvantage that the puppy can easily chew it and damage itself on protruding pieces of cane. The bed should be placed in a quiet, draught-free corner where the temperature is as even as possible. Draughts from the floor, which humans hardly notice, can be especially treacherous to a puppy, and it is therefore wise to select a bed with feet which raise it slightly from the

floor. But do not put the bed in an isolated position. A puppy is curious and wants to keep an eye on what is happening around it, and it also likes company. It will then quickly get used to all the usual sounds in the house. A door which slams at the least bit of draught, a gurgling sink, a droning fridge, a hissing pressure-cooker, not to mention blaring stereo equipment – there are many sounds in a home which can frighten an unprepared and lonely puppy out of his wits.

To make the puppy feel more secure in his new surroundings, the bed should be placed so that the puppy has its 'back free' – that is, nobody must be able to come from behind and frighten it. An unpleasant experience of that kind can make the dog simply refuse to go to the bed. Try from the very beginning to respect the puppy's own place. Just as you do not want it to jump up on your bed when you are having a lie-in, so the dog does not want to be disturbed when it is asleep. But be prepared for the fact that the puppy may

It doesn't need much to create a secure and comfortable bed

not share your own regular sleeping habits, as might be hoped. It may happen that in the middle of the night it decides to go and explore its new surroundings – this is more than likely because at that time it will be on its own. The easiest thing to prevent such nocturnal excursions is to buy a bed with such high sides that the puppy cannot climb over them. But you must count on waking up some time during the night to let the dog go to the toilet. As a rule, the puppy will accept that its freedom of movement is restricted – it will not imagine that being outside of its bed might be more fun. Don't put your dog on the lead in its bed, as it will experience the lead as a restriction which prevents it from partaking of all the excitement around the room. The result may be loud protests which will disturb your sleep. It is far better to put the bed beside your own for the first few nights so that you can give the puppy some reassurance in case it wakes up and starts to worry. Give it a cushion or a blanket as well so that it can 'make its bed' as it wants to. Lying directly on a plastic or vinyl-covered surface is not particularly comfortable for your puppy.

You must also arrange a fixed eating place for the newcomer, preferably in an undisturbed corner. Even if the puppy devours food in a couple of seconds – another habit which indicates that the dog is a direct descendant of the wolf – it is important that it is left alone while eating.

Fresh water must always be available and meals should be served at regular times. Choose the bowls with care. A cocker spaniel, for instance, cannot eat out of a wide bowl – its ears are too long and end up in the food. A greedy puppy which loves crawling into the bowl in order to get as much food as possible needs very stable bowls, or its water and food get spread all over the floor. Plastic bowls are both easy to wash up and cheap to buy but have the disadvantage that they scratch easily and a lot of bacteria settles in

Food bowls like this are impossible to knock over

the scratches. It is therefore better to spend more on stainless steel bowls.

Somewhere to sleep and somewhere to eat, peace and quiet for exploring a new world, love, consistency and patience – that is what is necessary to make your puppy feel welcome in its new home and settle there happily.

Another important point is that your puppy must have a name. If you have bought a registered puppy, it will have been given an 'official' name when it was registered by the breeder, a name which might be both long and convoluted. This name has to be used at shows, for breeding and so on, but if you do not like to use it every day you may choose whatever name you want. Start using it as soon as you pick up your chosen puppy for the first time. The name must always be associated with pleasure. Repeat it over and over again in a low, friendly voice. Never use it in combination with 'bad' when you need to correct the puppy. And if you let the name be accompanied by a pat and a little treat in the beginning, it will not be long before the puppy recognises it. It goes without saying that you always use it when you give your dog food.

Your dog's name should be short and preferably of two syllables, which makes it easy to call. It is good if it contains the letter S, which is easily recognised by dogs. Do not choose a very common name, however. Certain dogs' names, like children's names, are more popular and it is not good if three or four dogs come running when you call yours. Some people choose funny names for their dogs, but remember that you might have to use the name in the middle of a crowd if your dog has gone absent without leave, and it might not be quite so amusing to call it in that situation.

Love, care, patience, consistency – every chapter in this book ought really to end with these four words. They are essentials for your puppy to feel welcome in your house – and essentials under all circumstances when sharing a home with dogs.

Love is an amazing thing – it gets doubled if it's shared . . .

THE IMPORTANCE OF A COMMON LANGUAGE

As soon as possible after you bring your dog home, you must establish a good social relationship with it, a relationship or interplay that is based on mutual understanding and that will enable you both to trust each other. It is important to remember that *you* always set the limits of what is allowed and what is not allowed in the relationship and also with respect to other people and dogs; these limits must be consistently applied and every transgression must result in some kind of unpleasantness for the dog. But it is of utmost importance that you praise your dog when it does keep to the rules you have established.

Therefore you and your dog must develop a common language, a common signals system, in which the limits are defined. It is best if one member of the family is in charge of training – tone of voice, expression and body language can vary to such an extent between

You can say 'I like you' in many ways, but never often enough

various family members that the dog would only get confused – and later the rest of the family can participate in the learning together.

The aim of this book is to enable you to have a dog which 'functions' in our ever more complicated environment – not a circus dog that can perform cute tricks nor a show dog that fills your shelf with magnificent cups. The aim is rather to make the dog do what you want and participate on your terms, because it likes to and because it likes you. That is why praise for each success is so important, and much more important than the unpleasantness which follows failure. The fact is that failure is often caused by you rather than your dog.

Among the four special words I have used before – love, care, patience, and consistency – the latter is all-important when it comes to training. The dog learns by experience what is right and wrong, but it does not understand the difference between the two concepts. It must undergo, therefore, the same experience every time a specific thing happens or is about to happen. A dog cannot 'think' as we understand the word – not logically and definitely not in stages. It is easy to overestimate the dog's ability to think, to take an anthropomorphic approach to its way of reacting. It has no 'sense of ego' nor memory as we know it. That is why it serves no purpose to reproach or punish a dog for something that has already happened. It cannot think 'I did it, it was forbidden and that's why Daddy smacked my behind. I must not do it again.' This is why one must prevent a wrong action rather than punish the dog after it has done it. A dog has no 'moral sense' in human terms, it can't differentiate between obedience and disobedience.

It does not empty a bowl of sugar which has been left out because it is a thief; it does it because it thinks sugar tastes wonderful. A dog does not "abandon" the pack leader when he runs off after a bitch on heat – he

Sometimes, you just don't feel like paying attention . . .

just follows his instincts. A dog cannot be ashamed, repent or draw conclusions, but it knows the difference between pleasure and discomfort, and all training is built on this fact. It can learn to interpret signals but does not know what the words mean in themselves. For example, on the command 'Get the slippers', you can get it to do just that, but you can also train it to do the same by using the words 'Boil the potatoes', as long as you do it consistently. A dog cannot interpret separate words or place them in new contexts and that is why, all the time, you must use short, clear signals. If you happen to find your dog having a highly satisfactory chew of your favourite slippers, you can get it to stop with a sharp 'Bad'. Maybe not the first time but, if you repeat it enough times when you find your dog doing something which is not allowed, it will recognise that you are displeased with what it is doing and, as it is concerned both with your approval and its own welfare (which should amount to the same thing), it will soon stop. But if you tell it 'Bad' the first time, 'Stop' the second

time and the third time 'I've told you...', it does not understand a thing. Although it probably hears from your tone of voice that you are displeased, it only gets confused because it cannot grasp that different expressions mean the same thing. But bad memory does not mean that the dog cannot interpret several signals in a row. One can get it to perform very complicated tasks by giving it several pieces of information (signals and stimuli) that later can be reduced to one or two as the dog progressively becomes better trained.

If you understand clearly all the time that your dog is at the level of a child who has not learnt yet to talk and that you must use the same signals with the dog as with the child, then you will not have any problems communicating with your pet.

Besides this, there is also a completely different 'language' which dogs use among themselves, a body language which you can learn too, and use in teamwork with your dog (see pp 46 - 7).

UPBRINGING AND TRAINING

Is there really any difference between the two concepts? Maybe not. But we can count as upbringing the elementary skills all dogs must learn. First and foremost the puppy must be house-trained, and then it must learn to recognise its name, to get used to the lead, to be quiet, especially during the night, not to chew surrounding fixtures and fittings, to be able to be on its own without disturbing the neighbours, not to jump on the furniture, not to beg at the table, not to rush barking towards strangers, not to jump up on people, and so on – in short, 'to behave like a well-brought up human being would'.

These requirements ought to be considered as a matter of course, regardless of breed, where it lives, who looks after it and what its

functions might otherwise be – requirements which far too many dog owners neglect to teach their dogs.

As a rule, it is easy to turn a puppy into a socially well-adjusted and acceptable family member. With patience and consistency, it is often enough to build on the 'pleasure/unpleasantness principle'. The combination of praise and a treat is unbeatable as a teaching aid and is what we first and foremost recommend in this book. It is considerably more effective than the unpleasantness method, even if you may have to resort to this sometimes. If the dog is made to understand that you disapprove of what it is doing, then that is enough. The feeling of unpleasantness is released by a clear 'Bad' (spoken sharply), in worse cases by a light tug at the lead and in

No democratic vote about where the walk is taking us – you decide!

30

A firm grip at the scruff of the neck, without shaking, is a very effective way of saying, 'I don't like what you're doing!'. This is the language that the pup's dam uses, too

the very worst cases by taking the dog by the scruff of the neck in a calm and firm manner – without shaking it, though. That is how the female wolf corrects her cubs when they are up to some mischief.

The main thing is to take early action to prevent the formation of bad habits, both early in the life of a puppy and also promptly during the act. It happens only too frequently that a dog is corrected when it is too late. A dog functions very similarly to a child. It first has an impulse to do something – and a great many things can cause a dog to act impulsively – and then action follows. It is up to you to intervene just before the dog acts.

By careful observation of the puppy's be-

haviour you will soon find out what causes the impulsive actions you do not like, and this knowledge will give you time to intervene. But it is no use reproaching or correcting your dog after the action. Some people use the word 'No' to tell the dog that it is doing something forbidden. But having a common language is not enough – each expression must always mean the same thing.

Let me explain. In a big family, especially with a couple of teenagers, it happens fairly often that somebody shouts 'No' to indicate unwillingness in some context or other. If the dog is busy eating or settling down in its basket, a conflict will occur. It does not understand that the shout concerns somebody else, but thinks that what, until now, has not only been allowed, but even been praiseworthy, suddenly is being forbidden, which is completely incomprehensible to it. Say 'Bad' instead when you want your dog to understand that you disapprove of its intentions or of what it is already doing. That expression, after all, is not commonly used between family members. But the main thing is to be consistent.

It might sound negative, but the word 'Bad' is probably the most important word in the language you and your puppy have in common. Praise is, of course, most important. Without praise and approval, learning takes much longer. 'Bad' is the word that is going to explain to your puppy that you disapprove of what it is doing (or intends to do). When you have established your superior position in the puppy's hierarchy, the puppy will be very keen to have your approval, but it must also be made to know what you disapprove of: this is best done by using a terse, firm 'Bad', preferably underlined by a clear stop signal. It is always best that a prohibition is followed by an alternative – something that the dog is allowed to do instead – and gets lots of praise when it does it correctly. How do you teach your dog to understand this important word? It is not very difficult. On the next page you will find a simple method. You probably will not have to repeat the exercise many times before the puppy understands what it is about. As previously mentioned, it wants your approval.

1 Hold the puppy by the collar and put some dog treats in the grass

2 When it tries to get to the treats, stop it, saying 'Bad' and raising your right hand

3 Pull back the puppy a short distance, still with your hand raised, and repeat 'Bad'

4 Wait until the puppy relaxes and does not pull ahead. It can take from a couple of seconds to a couple of minutes (patience!). Then make an inviting gesture, at the same time saying 'There you are'. It is up to you to decide when the puppy is to be allowed to take the dog treat

When you are teaching your puppy the elementary skills, do not keep at it for so long that it stops being fun for both of you (except, of course, for toilet training). All training must be pleasant, a game in which you are in perfect harmony, trusting each other and getting on well together. Remember that a harsh word on the wrong occasion can spoil weeks of hard work. The dog cannot understand why you get irritated when things are not going according to plan. It is eager for your approval and does its best, but a dog can get tired too. Remember that the little puppy has to learn a lot in a short time. It has to learn several things at the same time, so it is doubly important that your signals to your dog – your common language – are clear and consistent.

House-training

The first, and most important, thing in your dog's education is to get it house-trained. 'Spending a penny' on the first day, out of pure fear of its new surroundings, is quite excusable, but you must, as mentioned before, intervene quickly. The critical moments occur when the dog has just woken, eaten or played. If you quickly take it outside and let it perform its business, giving it lots of praise the moment it has finished, preferably combined with a dog treat, then it will soon learn and try to earn your approval. In the beginning, you should always take the dog to the same spot.

Starting to teach your dog to go to a sheet of paper or to use the floor drain in the bathroom just means that it will take twice as long to house-train your pet, because you have to train it twice – you would not want your dog to continue using paper and the bathroom for ever! Rome was not built in one day, however, and you must be prepared to wipe up for a while – an accident happens easily. Saying 'Bad' the moment you discover that something is about to happen and moving the dog outside equally speedily – where praise is waiting, if all goes well – is the simplest method of getting a dog house-trained. It is important in this context to get the timing right so that the dog does not connect your 'Bad' with relieving its bladder and go into hiding when it feels the urge. The sign

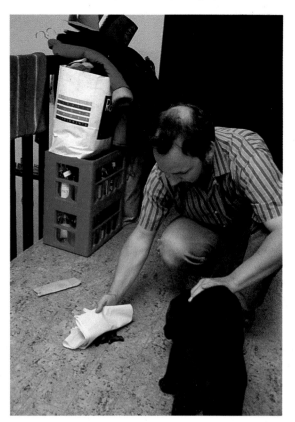

Accidents will happen . . .

that communications have gone wrong is when you find the result behind the sofa or hidden somewhere else. Most puppies become house-trained without their owners having to resort to saying 'Bad'.

A sure sign that the moment has come for the puppy to go outside is when it starts to move around in circles while sniffing intensely, and it is then time to intervene. But this strange circling habit can also mean that the dog is tired and wants to go to bed. The only difference is that they do not sniff as eagerly when they want to go to bed as they do when they need to go out. Many wild animals trample an even bed in the grass or the snow before they lie down. The trampling also serves to frighten away snakes, for example, or other animals that might disturb their sleep.

It is hard work, but getting a puppy house-trained within two or three months or so should not be any great problem. By then, it has learned the lesson and gives a signal of its own accord by whining at the door or scratching it, for example, when it wants to go out – and this should earn your praise. In autumn and winter, it can take a little longer to house-train your dog. It is understandable that some dogs do not find relieving themselves out in the cold particularly enjoyable and that their discomfort is greater than your admonishing 'Bad', so they choose to do it inside instead.

This might be the time to remind you again that a dog does not have a particularly long memory. If you discover in the morning that an accident has happened during the night, saying 'Bad' is useless. The dog does not remember what it did during the night and does not understand why you have re-proached it. It might also be your fault – for example, was it too much of a bother to take the dog out in the bad weather the previous evening? In that case you should blame your-self. In order to avoid that kind of accident, it is best to take the dog out every night before bedtime, preferably at the same time and to the same spot, and do not give it anything to drink after that.

There are those who consider themselves authorities on dogs, who still insist that the best way to punish a dog for an 'accident' is to rub its sensitive nose in it, on the assump-tion that a dog will never forget such a les-son. Such an 'authority' should not have a dog.

Attentiveness, quickness, firmness and consistency – these are the qualities which count.

Answering to its name

Finding a good name for the new member of the family is not enough – it must answer to it as well. As a rule this involves no problems. Just make sure that the puppy thinks there is nothing better than coming when it is called. After you have called your dog by name, pat it as soon as it comes up to you, praise it and preferably give it a dog treat. It is recom-mended that you squat and that you are alone with your dog when you start to teach it to answer to its name. Your voice comes from very far above and it can be difficult to identify who called if several persons are present. If you move away slowly while call-ing its name, the dog's curiosity will double.

When the dog begins to understand the lesson you are teaching it, you can start to make things more difficult, thereby impress-ing the dog's name on its memory even more. Hide behind a tree, for example, when the dog is not paying attention, and as soon as you see that it is getting worried, having discovered that it has lost its pack leader, step forward and call it by repeating its name sev-eral times. In this case use only praise. But if your dog is a softy, you must be careful with this kind of exercise. You must never re-proach or punish a dog even if you have to wait until your patience is exhausted. Why should your dog ever come back to you then? It risks something unpleasant. Never chase a dog if it does not come at once. You will either frighten it to death, or it will think of it as a great game, and then you might have to chase it every time you let it off the

From the very beginning, you must show the puppy how you want things done. You have to do this in a firm, friendly and consistent way

34

lead. Furthermore there is no purpose in doing this. However fast you are, a short-legged dachshund is faster and fitter than you.

Never put your dog on the lead the moment it comes to you. According to the logic of a dog that is playing, your call means that the fun is over – and that, of course, is right. If you must put the dog on the lead straight away for some reason, make it as pleasant as possible by giving it a treat the moment the lead is on.

The dog should think that nothing is nicer than coming to you when it is called. Nothing should be able to lure it away from you, not chasing cats or birds, not playing with other dogs, not exciting or interesting smells – nothing. That is why it is so important that you always receive your dog with open arms and praise it when it comes, even if, in the beginning, you might have to wait a while before it comes. If you have to call it too many times your voice will get irritated, which the dog interprets as a sign of your displeasure. Your displeasure usually means

There are many situations in which you must have your dog under your complete control, as both these pictures show

unpleasantness, so, in that case, why should it come? It is important to sound happy and friendly, even if it is difficult.

Having a dog which is obedient in all situations is the definite confirmation of the trust between you, because the dog, by coming, recognises that you are pack leader, and it also knows that compliance means something pleasant, since you praise it for coming.

Getting used to the lead

Having a collar put on and being hooked to a lead is something which a happy and curious puppy sees as an unpleasant occurrence, robbing it of its liberty. That is why it is important to proceed carefully and keep the lessons short.

Start with putting the collar on for a short while. It is not as easy as it seems. Naturally, the puppy wonders what it is all about and might even try to bite the collar. Do not then be tempted to grab the puppy's nose and force the collar over its head. The dog will experience the grip around its nose as something very unpleasant and try to tear itself free. Talk instead to the puppy in a

The collar will in the end help the pup to feel secure

friendly manner, try to distract it in some way and sneak on the collar without it noticing. If it starts to scratch at the collar with its hind legs or tries to bite it, continue to speak kindly to it and give it a dog treat or try to distract its attention in some other way. It will soon forget the collar and accept that it has to wear one.

Then it is time to put a lead on the puppy. Try not to let it notice that the lead means restraint. Let it decide both where to go and at what pace; let the lead hang loosely the whole time.

After a couple of such lessons you can take over the command. Begin by squatting and carefully pulling the puppy towards you with the lead, at the same time praising it and giving it a treat when it has come to you. Repeat this several times. After that you may start to walk it on the lead. Get it used to walking on your left side from the beginning and keep its attention the whole time by making friendly noises and praising it. Remember that at this stage the only thing that matters is getting the puppy used to its collar and lead and to get it to walk approximately in the direction you want. The lead is essential for controlling your dog when you are out together. In case the puppy suddenly stops or pulls very hard, you must in no way try any harsh correction methods. Just sit down, call the dog and start all over again.

Walking your dog off the lead is something to which we shall return later.

Keeping quiet

Few things have disturbed good relations between neighbours than barking dogs. In a block of flats it is especially a sensitive matter. A dog that throws itself, madly barking, against the door whenever it hears footsteps outside, or a lift door being shut or a door bell – and it might be somebody else's door – can drive anybody to a nervous breakdown. It is fortunate that not all dogs are door barkers.

Barking is, of course, a manifestation of the dog's instinct to defend itself and its territory, but it is a nuisance which you must try to prevent as early as possible. It is time consuming and you might even have to sacrifice a few days of your holidays to stay at home

You must be able to leave the dog alone without it disturbing the neighbours

and devote yourself to solving this problem. It certainly is a problem and it gets worse the longer you put off doing something about it.

The dog's reaction is always triggered by certain stimuli – in this case a certain noise outside the door – and you always have that short reaction time to try to intervene. A dog's hearing is infinitely better than yours, and it usually first reacts to a sound by lifting its head and turning it towards the source of the sound, pricking its ears. If the sound is weak, the dog does not interpret it as a threat and does not start to bark immediately. That is your chance to intervene. The best way is to get the dog to think of something else and thus make it forget the sound. Throw an object – for example, a newspaper or a small ball – after it or, in the worst cases, at it, and at the same time give a short, sharp 'Quiet' and then call the dog to you, caress it and praise it if it keeps quiet until the noise outside the door has finished.

It is slightly more difficult to get the dog

to stop barking if somebody rings the bell or knocks at the door. It is best to do this training together with another member of the family. Ask somebody go outside and ring the door bell. Sit down close to the dog and say 'Quiet' before it has time to start barking. Grab the collar and let it accompany you to the door when you go to open it. Tell it to be quiet the moment it shows any inclination to get noisy. Praise it if it is quiet when you open the door. If you repeat this several times, the dog will get used to the fact that well-intentioned people have rung the bell, and it will simply stop caring about the sound of the bell. You can reinforce this behaviour by asking friends and acquaintances to bring some treat for the dog when they come to see you, and to hand it over as soon as you open the door to let them in.

Your door-bell should not ring too loudly and you should ask your visitors not to knock too hard on the door. Such sudden loud noises can frighten anybody, and a frightened dog will forget all your admonitions and bark incessantly. Change the door-bell and the problem will solve itself.

Dogs which bark and howl the moment they are left alone at home are also a great infliction on the neighbourhood. This behaviour is perfectly understandable. A puppy is the object of everybody's interest, and, if suddenly left alone, it will wonder what is happening.

Start by leaving your dog on its own for only a minute or two in another room – preferably in the room where it usually sleeps – for a short while after returning from a good long walk, so that it will be tired. Put the dog in its bed, say the word 'Down' and go out of the room, leaving the door ajar. Wait outside and go in again as soon as the dog shows any inclination to get up and leave its bed. Make it lie down again, repeating 'Down'. Prolong little by little your stay outside. A dog that feels secure, and a little tired, will soon get used to being on its own in 'its' room, and if the bed is comfortable it will soon fall into a quiet sleep.

It is important to be able to see if the puppy is afraid or simply cautious

It is somewhat more difficult to get the puppy used to being alone in the house or flat. But with the help of this preliminary training, it should not cause any problems. Slip away without the puppy noticing – for example when it is eating, and preferably when it is a little tired. It does not really know where to look for you, and it will certainly not sit down by the door and howl. Watch it through a window or through the letterbox and go back in before it gets too worried. Praise it if it kept quiet while you were out. Then stay away longer, but go back again before the dog gets worried. There is after all a certain logic to the dog's reaction. It has discovered that you are back before it starts to feel lonely and insecure, so why should it worry?

If your dog starts to bark or whine before you come back, a moment of unpleasantness is needed. Open the door quickly and show your disapproval with a sharp 'Bad'. There are those who advocate a somewhat harsher method – for example, throwing a wet rag through a window at the barking puppy. That might be rather drastic but perhaps it must be used as a last resort. You must under all circumstances be able to leave your dog alone at home, without it becoming an insoluble problem.

Knowing its place

A dog is certainly good company but not everywhere and not all the time. Certain places – for example, soft furniture, your own bed and maybe the nursery – should be prohibited territory. There is in general no difficulty in getting the dog to understand where it is allowed and not allowed to go. Saying 'Bad' when it is straying from the right path is usually enough, but most important is that you are consistent. Having a soft dog as bed-warmer in case the boiler breaks down can be very comfortable indeed, but in that case you will have to take into account that your dog will jump up on your soft, comfortable bed when it comes back after a walk in the rain. Allowing your dog to do something once means that it will always be permitted. Dogs are logical creatures. Besides, if your dog goes with you when you visit somebody, that somebody might be less than pleased about your pet wandering around everywhere and jumping up on the furniture. It is therefore important to make the rules clear to the dog.

No begging!

It is not pleasant to have a dog that begs at the table. Make it a habit to feed your dog before you have your own meal, in which case the problem should not occur. A dog that is full does not need to beg for food. Do not be tempted to give it something at the table, however pleadingly it might look at you, but shoo it away, firmly but kindly and – sorry to nag – consistently.

Sometimes you both need to take a break from one another, and the 'dog-free' area of the house is a good place of retreat

All puppies are born with the need to chew, shake, pull and bite

No chewing the furniture and fixtures

Being a dog is sometimes boring. It feels better if there is something to do, something to chew – a rug, for example, or a shoe or the leg of a table. Just like a child, a puppy can have teething troubles, with a terrible itch, and chewing something makes it feel better. But mischief chewing is mainly a consequence of lack of stimulation, so the dog's bad habit is mainly your own fault. Play with the dog, keep it occupied, talk to it, let it be with you as much as possible – and that is on the whole why one gets a dog. But if you leave it to amuse itself, it is best to give it some suitable 'toys' and remove all the other items which invite chewing. The best thing is

a chew of ox-hide that you can buy in your local pet shop. You can also get advice there on which toys are suitable and which will not harm your dog. Otherwise, the usual rule applies: intervene before any damage is done by uttering a disapproving 'Bad' and give the dog a permitted toy, praising it when it takes that toy instead. If the dog has, unbeknown to you, selected its own chewing place (they return frequently to the 'scene of the crime'), you can rub that place with something which does not smell particularly pleasant and which will irritate the dog's nose. But be careful, dogs have sensitive noses.

How to stop your dog chasing cars and bicycles

This is not just a bad habit, it is also a dangerous one, so your dog must be quickly cured of it. Find out if your dog has any such inclinations by asking somebody to slowly drive past it in a car or on a bicycle. If the dog tries to chase after the car or bicycle, pull it back with a short firm jerk of the lead, backing it up by saying 'Bad'.

Try also when the dog is off the lead. Then, if it gives chase, have the cyclist or a passenger in the car (through an open door) give it a smack with a loosely folded paper or throw a jug of water over it. After one or two experiences of this kind, most dogs will stop chasing vehicles.

How to stop your dog charging at and jumping up on people

It is difficult to get a dog to stop doing this, since it is its natural way of greeting people and showing its pleasure. This behaviour goes back to the 'wolf stage'. When the wolf mother returns to the lair, the pups jump up and try to reach the corners of her mouth in order to induce her to regurgitate the half-digested contents of her stomach, which is their chief diet. In this case, punishing the dog for what we consider unsuitable behaviour does not help, but we must prevent it and offer an alternative before resorting to an unpleasant experience. Breaking the habit must take place in two stages. Have a dog treat ready when the dog comes rushing, hold it out and wait for a short while before you let the dog take it. Then squat and say hello to the dog. Turn your head away a little as the dog might interpret direct eye contact as aggressiveness on your part, which might be intensified if you smile – after all, you do show your teeth when you smile. In this way, you are meeting on the same level.

This exercise must be repeated many times, because, as mentioned earlier, it goes against the natural behaviour of the dog. The next stage will be to express your displeasure with a 'Bad' as soon as the dog shows an inclination to jump up, and to push it down firmly. There is also a harder school which advocates putting a knee lightly in the chest of the jumping dog, but, since the dog often comes running at a high speed, there is a risk that it can be badly injured. It might also become scared of greeting people at all.

If it is necessary to resort to an unpleasant experience to put an end to the dog's habit of jumping up at people, you can use the method which is described on the next page. It has the advantage of not making the dog feel that you are causing the unpleasantness but that it is self-inflicted, so to speak. It is a very effective method.

Not everyone appreciates a dog's affection . . .

1 The dog handler puts his foot on the lead surreptitiously

2 When the dog jumps up it is pulled straight back by the short lead

3. Squat and make a fuss of the puppy so that it does not connect the unpleasantness with you but with the actual jump, since it is pulled back, apparently not by you, as it tries to jump up

It might be worth pointing out that you must protect the puppy from people who rush up at it. Few people can resist a sweet puppy and most take it for granted that they are allowed to stroke it. Since it is only a puppy and you might not have got it under proper control, you must learn to say 'No' in these situations.

You are responsible for the puppy, and you will never know what it might do if it gets over-excited because of the fuss or becomes frightened by a stranger's outstretched hand (and teeth, if the stranger smiles at the puppy!). That is why you must gently but firmly refuse when somebody tries to stroke your puppy. This does not mean that you must protect your puppy from all contact with people other than your family, but you must limit it – at least in the beginning – to people both of you know.

Environmental training

As soon as you think that have some control over your dog, you must start to train it to get used to the environment. Make it a habit to take the dog with you as often as possible when you are going out somewhere, and let it gradually get accustomed to an increasingly difficult environment. If you live in a town, take the dog to the countryside – and the other way round.

'Wild animals', such as cows, horses and chickens, strong smells and large open spaces, or cars, street noises and milling crowds jostling for space – a dog must get used to many things, and it is best to start as early as possible – but not too early, as you don't want to cause it stress. Remember that you are the centre of the dog's life; you are the pack leader and must guarantee its safety. So keep the lead short, but not too short. Reversing is part of the puppy's survival mechanism, and too short a lead can make it panic. Talk to it calmly and encourage it, stroke it often, sit down and have a break

and let it look around and get used to its new environment. Let it sniff and investigate. This is part of the dog's absorption of its surroundings.

Do not fuss over the dog if it gets frightened or, worse, pushed and trod on. It does not understand your words but it can hear from your tone of voice that what happened was really frightening. (It might have been, of course, but if you transfer your fear to your dog, it might have a lasting effect and then everything becomes suddenly dangerous.) In that case your dog might not gain the self-confidence it needs. Calm it instead, distract it from what has frightened it and stroke it, speaking words of encouragement the whole time.

If, in the beginning, your dog ever panics and forges ahead on the lead or sits down and refuses to go further, do not get impatient and do not scold it. It is not perfect behaviour on the lead or disciplined walking to heel which is most important at that time. Instead, let it come to you, calm it, guide it past the danger and then continue as if noth-

The world is full of unknown monsters . . .

ing has happened. The ultimate goal is for you to have a harmonious, safe dog which you can take with you everywhere, a good companion that never causes you any trouble.

Going where you want it to

What was originally planned as a nice walk with your dog can quickly develop into single-handed combat, where the dog pulls madly in one direction and an increasingly desperate dog owner in the other. There are so many distractions that might invite a puppy to choose a path other than the one you want: other dogs, for instance. They have a well-established language when they want to establish contact with each other. They can challenge each other to a fight, invite to play, mark their territory or send signals of insecurity. Or birds, cats, cars, cyclists, smells, a fluttering leaf, a rustling sound – a puppy's world is full of temptations. That is why it is you who has to decide when to stop, when to continue – ignoring all the many temptations – and in which direction to go.

1 Before you start, place a pleasant-smelling dog treat on the lawn. Then, with the puppy on the lead, walk slowly past it.

This is a crucial point in establishing the hierarchy within the pack and in confirming you as leader – even if the pack consists only of you and the puppy. When the pecking order has been established, it will last for ever. Here you must use a combination of a well-developed body language and your voice and – as always, equally important – praise when all goes well

2 The moment the puppy starts to pull towards its bowl, you pull it towards you (do not tug at the lead), at the same time saying 'Bad'. On no account must you let the dog get so close to the bowl that it succeeds in snatching a treat

3 Continue pulling the puppy towards you and indicate with a gesture which way to go

4 Praise the puppy and talk to distract its attention as soon as it has lost interest in the food bowl and follows you instead. How to learn right and left turns is shown on p 80-1

45

Your dog's body language becomes clear in the company of other dogs

To be with other dogs

You must never let your dog show aggressiveness towards other dogs. It is your own fault if it does so. You might, of course, have acquired a dog with bad, that is, aggressive, inclinations, but the risk is minimal if you have bought it from a breeder of good reputation. The cause of aggressiveness is usually wrong training.

That is why contact with other dogs, especially in the beginning, must take place under supervision. But you must also control yourself. When, as a new dog owner walking your dog, you meet another dog, it is easy in apprehension to pull the lead towards you, thus pulling your dog's head and shoulders back, which is an aggressive signal. Further, your apprehension could transfer to your puppy, making its hackles rise and causing it to bark. All this challenges the oncoming dog, which answers in kind, and the fun and games begin.

Relax instead. Pretend that the other dog is not there and distract your puppy by talking calmly to it, so that it feels safe close to you and does not need to issue a challenge or frighten away the other dog, which it might not have even noticed. Praise it when the danger is past. If, in spite of this, it makes a lunge, pull the lead, say 'Close' and continue walking. Praise it when it calms down and walks by your side once more. ('Close' has been used as a command rather than 'Heel' because it is easier to make 'Heel' into an unpleasant and aggressive sound, which the puppy might interpret negatively, than it is 'Close'.)

You often hear dog owners say 'But my dog only wants to play... And a grown-up dog never hurts a puppy'. That a happy, impulsive puppy off the lead rushes up to an older dog has nothing to do with aggressiveness. It is only curious and playful, but you should know that it is not entirely without risk. It is true that the older dog does not think of your puppy's advances as a threat, but not all dogs like being disturbed and might 'correct' the puppy in a rough manner. This is why you must never let your puppy off the lead if there are other, unknown dogs around. Also, if it has started to leave puppyhood, an advance can be seen as a threat, as hierarchy competition, and in a trice a fight could begin.

As mentioned previously, all contact with other dogs must take place under supervision – that is, you must never let your dog, when on the lead, try to establish contact with a strange dog off the lead. They must only be in direct contact if both are on the lead. You must, of course, ask the other dog owner if he has any objection to the dogs 'saying hello'. Dogs have a well-developed body language which shows their intentions and how they see themselves and each other, a language which you must learn to understand – and, to a certain extent, 'speak' yourself.

During the first few minutes, when the dogs sniff each other carefully, the signals are usually particularly clear and that is when you must keep your eyes on them. Aggressiveness can be released quicker than you think.

If all goes well, as it frequently does, especially if the dogs are of different sex, one can just let them content themselves with a short greeting ceremony; maybe you can then make an appointment with the owner to meet somewhere where the dogs can run off the lead. Puppies, like children, need playmates.

If, as luck would have it, there is a proper dog fight, there are effective methods to end it. Grab the base of the tail firmly and pull the dog away. The discomfort is enough to make the dog lose all interest in continuing the fight. Another way is to grab a hind leg, lift it and pull it back, but any restraint must be applied to both dogs or you will risk putting your dog at a disadvantage by breaking down his defences. However, if your dog is well brought up there is no risk of this kind of situation arising.

If the rough and tumble becomes serious, you must be prepared to intervene quickly

CHILDREN AND DOGS

Children and dogs warrant a chapter by themselves. How many parents have not fallen for 'I promise to look after it myself...' or 'Looking after a dog is not difficult at all. Lots of my friends have one...'. The truth of the matter is that no child is capable of having the sole responsibility of looking after a dog. A dog must be the concern of the whole family, but an adult must have the final responsibility. Quarrelling about who is going to take the dog out on a chilly autumn evening when there is something thrilling on TV makes neither dog nor man happy. Arguments like 'It is your dog so you must take it out...' or 'You wanted it, so you take it out...' are futile. On the other hand, having a dog and looking after it can unite the family through a common interest.

Children simply cannot cope physically with a big dog. They cannot possibly intervene if there is a crisis. A dog that exceeds 20lb (9kg) can drag a ten-year-old 'dog handler' wherever it wants to go. A warning is pertinent here. Enterprising, or dog-mad, children sometimes offer to walk the dog, especially in cities. Do not be tempted to let them out alone, but do let them accompany you when you walk your dog. The more children the dog gets to know, the safer it becomes with children. Also, let your own children learn to control and handle the family dog as soon as it is trained.

The combination of small – really small – children and dogs usually causes no problems. Most dogs have a high level of tolerance as far as children are concerned. Certain

Children and dogs seem to find a common language very quickly

breeds – for instance, labradors – are very patient with children, and there is no doubt that patience can be needed, because in most cases it is more than likely that the child is troublesome to the dog and, if the games become too wild or too prolonged, even the most patient dog can tire. If it does, it is possible that it will indicate that it no longer wishes to join in. Even a puppy has the right to be left alone, however sweet and gentle it may be, particularly when it is eating or sleeping, and it must definitely never be treated as a toy. It is your responsibility as a parent to teach this to the child.

Many people believe that the reverse is more difficult – to introduce a new baby into a dog-owning family. Sometimes you hear terrible stories about jealous dogs which have attacked and occasionally even killed newborn children, but these are, in most cases, just stories. Of course, there are mentally disturbed dogs that could do this, but a normal dog has built-in barriers against attacking children. If you do not fuss too much over the new family member – in the eyes of the dog – all is usually well. Do not make any changes to the dog's world, however – for example, do not move its bed or close off areas where it usually moves freely, so that it feels isolated. Of course, a dog, even if it is not jealous, can feel abandoned and that is just as bad. If the dog is allowed to acquaint itself with the new baby and is not driven away – for instance, during nursing times – and if its life remains basically unaltered from what it was previously, there is no risk of complications.

It is always you, as an adult, who have the responsibility for the development of the relationship between child and dog. If that relationship develops the right way, it can be a source of infinite happiness to all concerned. Children who do not have the opportunity to grow up with dogs miss a lot.

Dogs and children can never have enough love

DOG LANGUAGE

The tails show clearly which dog is dominant and which is inferior

Communication between you and your dog is not just one-way, owner to dog. Your pet needs to communicate with you, too. Every dog has a great and legitimate need to talk to its owner, a wish to make itself understood, which you must respect and which, if you learn to interpret the 'language' correctly, can mean much for your mutual trust and interplay. It is not that easy but, by observing how dogs 'talk' to each other, one can learn much. The dog has made an impact on man for thousands of years – it sees man as a pack member – and it gives on the whole the same signals to man as it does to fellow canines.

We sometimes find a dog's signals very difficult to interpret and often they seem ambiguous – a little child once said of a tail-wagging barking dog that it was happy at one end and angry at the other. We associate tail-wagging with friendliness and happiness, but, strangely enough, it can also imply a threat and can express that the dog considers itself dominant. The bark can mean happiness, as well as warning and uncertainty – it depends entirely on the tone of voice.

The most important means of expression are the face and head, the tail and the posture. It is these we must learn to interpret. Watch what happens when two dogs meet and see how their contact develops. This will give you the best possible dog-language vocabulary.

If the dogs know each other, the dominant dog has its ears raised and the corners of its mouth in the normal position, while the subordinate dog lays its ears back and pulls back the corners of its mouth. By this the order of rank is determined and there is nothing more to 'talk about'.

Dogs sometimes resort to coarser language if they do not know each other. Both bare their teeth, but it is not the dominant dog that shows most. The submissive dog keeps its ears back and the corners of its mouth back, showing most teeth, which is not what you would expect. In order to avoid a violent end to the meeting, the dominant dog tries to diminish the other's aggressiveness by turning away its head momentarily, An adult dog might do that when it meets a puppy. It was believed previously that it was the submissive dog which turned its head – 'turning the other cheek' – which might well be interpreted as unconditional surrender. That is a mistake – which is confirmed when we observe how the social behaviour of the two dogs develops.

Dog language has its origin in the primeval dog, but man has deprived certain breeds of some of their means of expression through

Sometimes, dog language can be coarse . . .

Would you like to play?

breeding and other interference – for example, docked ears and tails are not as expressive as natural ones, and the tail of a spitz which lies curved over its back is not demonstrative in the same way as the tail of an alsatian, so we can only talk in terms of a 'normal tail'. A quiet, well-balanced dog in an unthreatening environment keeps its tail hanging loosely in a slight curve. If it is friendly, it will wave it vigorously. If it is really sociable, the whole hind quarters will sometimes follow. A threatening dog, which tries to dominate, lifts its tail straight up and, in order to make this even more clear, it sometimes waves it rapidly and stiffly. The dog often raises its hackles as well. On the other hand, the submissive dog will lower its tail or even put it between its legs.

Dogs have a well-developed body language. Stiff legs and strutting movements indicate aggressiveness as does a forward-tilting position of the body, while submission is signalled by bent legs and cringing movements

I don't want to play any more

– sometimes the dog will lie down and in extreme cases it will even lie on its back.

Here a warning would not be out of place. You must not let yourself be fooled by signals of submission. It does not mean that the dog is not dangerous – rather the contrary. A dog giving such signals is insecure and afraid and can snap quickly in order to defend itself. On the other hand, a dominant dog is not necessarily dangerous. He certainly challenges you, but if you act resolutely you can take over the dominating role. But independently of the signals the dog gives, the basic rule is that you should never touch strange dogs without the owner being present and giving his permission.

You and your dog will eventually develop your own language: the whimper by the door when it wants to go out, the scratching on the refrigerator door when it is hungry, the total deafness when it does not want the same thing as you, the bark of impatience when it has to wait too long for you to play with it, the friendly prodding to confirm that you are a chum, and so on. If you are sensitive, this can be developed into a means of communication between you that is both very varied and highly private.

There is specialist literature for those who want to know more about dog language, but the best method of learning it is always to look and listen carefully.

I want so much to understand!

TRANSPORTATION

General rules

There are different regulations in different countries on letting dogs travel by public transport. There are generally specially allocated areas on buses and trains where you are allowed to sit with a dog. In most countries you are not allowed to bring your pet with you into sleeping-cars, restaurant-cars or similar places. A small dog may accompany you as hand-luggage on the condition that it is kept in a cage or a basket, from which it cannot get out. As a general rule, the dog must be kept under control so that it does not disturb other passengers or foul the surroundings.

In an aircraft

When flying, the rule without exception is that dogs, at least moderately big ones, must be transported in special cages in the luggage compartment of the aircraft. In special cases a small dog, carried in a suitable bag on the knee, may be permitted. Check the rules before you travel.

On the bicycle

You sometimes see cyclists carrying even quite large dogs in a little box or on a specially constructed shelf on the bicycle. Obviously, it can be eye-catching, almost something of a circus act, but it is, of course, highly dangerous – both for the cyclist and for the dog. What happens if the dog jumps from the bicycle because it has become frightened or has caught sight of a cat? At best, it was loose in the box, and is only a danger to itself and the surrounding traffic; at worst, it is on a lead and the cyclist is deposited without further ado on the ground.

If you want to take the dog with you when you are cycling, it must run alongside. When you are taking the dog for a walk, you should

On buses, take care to protect your dog from being trampled on

A little dog can be kept in a basket or bag

Always get onto a bus before your dog, to make way for it

Bringing the pillow it usually has in its basket will help the dog to feel more secure and will keep it fairly calm. Fit a special luggage – or dog-guard, so that the dog cannot get into the back seat. If you have a normal car, you should fit such a guard between the front and the back seats. Never let the dog sit beside you in the front seat. If, for reason of space, you have no option but to keep the dog in front, you must put it on the floor by the passenger seat.

Many dogs will travel by car for a long distance without problem, while others suffer from travel sickness. Do not start a long journey or go on holiday immediately after you have acquired a puppy. It could be a disaster. There are special sickness pills for dogs, but in spite of these the journey could still be arduous. Slowly get the puppy used to the car and let it first go for short trips of an hour or so. Do not let it eat before the trip nor during it, provided the travelling time is not too long.

Heat is the biggest problem for a dog when travelling by car. The dog has sweat-

always keep it on your left side, but when you cycle you must always keep your bicycle between the dog and the other traffic. How you learn this together is shown on p109.

It is an excellent way to exercise your dog, but it has to suit its age and condition. Never go too far or so fast that the dog has to gallop. Asphalt wears down dog pads more than gravel, so you must be particularly careful when you cycle with your dog in town, for instance.

In a car

Dogs in a car can be a problem. An estate car or van is the best type of vehicle for transporting a dog. You can set aside a special place for your pet, and make up a bed with a soft cover or blanket on which it can lie down and stretch out properly. You should also give it something to occupy itself with – a bone to gnaw or suchlike – and talk to it now and then, because a dog, and particularly a puppy, can become rather trying if it is bored, which does not help traffic safety.

If you have to have the dog in front, keep it on the floor

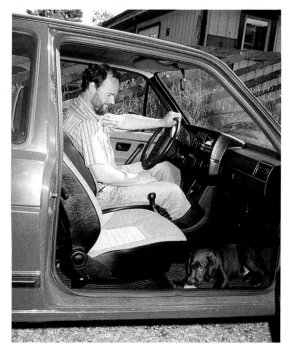

A familiar dog box will help the dog to feel more secure

glands only on the small pieces of skin between the pads and thus has difficulty in getting rid of surplus heat. It is usually said that a dog perspires with its tongue when it is panting, but that is often not enough. Therefore make sure that you have good ventilation for the dog without exposing it to draught. Sometimes you will see a driver letting his dog put its whole head through an open window while he is driving. Although it is nice and cool, the dog cannot understand the risk of inflammation to both eyes and ears which can be the result of a such a strong draught. It is up to the driver to take precautions.

Dark dogs in particular – the dark coat absorbs the heat – and snub-nosed dogs – they cannot pant away the surplus heat – have difficulties in summer. It is always advisable to take some thick terry towels and a large container of water in the car. If the dog gets too hot, you simply have to soak the towel and put it over the dog. In severe cases, you can pour the water straight over the animal. If it suffers badly from the heat, this action can save its life. If the worst comes to the worst and the dog faints due to the heat, immediately after attempting to cool it, you must find the nearest vet and let him treat your pet.

But such extreme cases are rare, and there is no risk of your dog fainting from heat if the ventilation is sufficient and you keep a careful eye on the dog, often stopping and taking it out for exercise and making sure that it has enough water to drink. It is a good idea to put up a sun screen on the windows. This could be to your advantage as well.

You should not leave the dog alone in a vehicle in the summer. If you have to leave your dog alone, make sure that one or two windows are kept open for ventilation and always park in the shade. Never leave a dog alone for long in a vehicle.

If you have a caravan or trailer, do not let the dog stay in it during the journey. You would not know how the dog was feeling or what it was up to and it could get hurt if you had to brake suddenly or take quick evasive action.

By boat

Dogs do not have an instinctive boat-sense, so the order 'Sit in boat' from the skipper will be unheeded if you do not have your dog under complete control. A dog might like to jump up and bark at a passing boat, especially if there is another dog on board, scratch itself or walk up to its owners to say hello. If you have a dog on board you must be prepared for sudden manoeuvres by the dog, otherwise the consequences can be catastrophic. It is also important that you match boat and dog, so to say – for example, a great dane and a canoe are not a good combination. For most dogs the boat is at worst a wildly rolling room that refuses to stay still and from which there is no escape. There is nowhere to go and a dog does not appreciate shining, varnished decks. If the deck is rolling a lot, the dog tries to brake with its claws, which may leave scratches and marks on a well-polished surface. As a dog cannot anticipate when the boat is about to lurch, it is best to keep it below decks, in a place with good ventilation. If you are particularly concerned about your dog scratching the varnished decks, you can make it wear shoes, of the type used when a dog has hurt a paw, and keep them tied on while it is on board. To be on the safe side, you could glue some ribbed rubber – for instance, a piece of a bicycle tyre – onto the soles.

If you let your dog stay with you on deck, you must fit it with a special life-vest with handles and preferably tie a lifeline to it – it is not the easiest thing to try to fish out a panicky dog that has fallen overboard. Make sure that the life-vest is fitted properly, otherwise the dog could turn upside down when it falls in the water. If the dog is on the lead onboard, use a harness. If you fasten the lead to the collar, it might strangle itself if it falls overboard.

Be prepared for your dog, happy to get away from the rolling surroundings, to jump towards the shore long before the boat has berthed and to swim the last stretch. Therefore, as the boat approaches the shore it is important to have the dog on the lead. A wet dog running around freely would not be particularly popular wherever you might land. Sunbathers on the beach or wildlife on the desolate skerry – all will be similarly disturbed by it. Furthermore, your dog can hurt itself seriously if it misses the jump and hits against a jetty or rock or the side of the boat.

There are special seasick pills for dogs, but if you notice that your dog cannot tolerate the sea very well, try to make alternative arrangements so that it does not have to accompany you on the boat. Remember the naval hero Admiral Nelson – who never got used to sailing and was seasick every time he went to sea. If you have to use seasick pills, first let the dog try them on shore. Some dogs are upset by pills and can react strongly.

With a familiar cushion or blanket and something to play with, most dogs manage car journeys quite well

Left If the dog falls in the water and is close to drowning, you must act quickly. Lift the dog up by the hind legs as soon as you have got it up on deck or on land to empty its lungs of water. Draw out its tongue so that it does not block the windpipe. Compress its chest with your knees – about fifteen times per minute if the dog is fully grown and somewhat quicker if it is a puppy – but take care that you do not injure it. Clean any slime from the mouth cavity and the throat, preferably asking somebody else to help so that you do not need to interrupt your action of pressing the chest.

Below and opposite Continue for a while and then put the dog on a hard surface and continue pressing the chest with one hand. With the other hand keep the dog's muzzle high and keep its tongue to one side. Press at the same rate all the time. This method can also be used to give heart massage to a dog that has collapsed, for instance by over-exertion or heat.

You must take the dog to the vet for after-care as soon as possible after it starts to breathe by itself.

TRAINING

WALKING ON THE LEAD

You do not need to see many dogs out for a walk before you realise that walking on the lead or walking to heel or 'Close' is one of the most important stages in the training of the dog. Too often it is the dog that drags or pulls its master or mistress, or the other way around, and it is definitely not a pleasant sight. If the dog-handler desperately jerks and pulls the lead in order to determine, at least to a certain degree, where the panting dog should go, this could be close to cruelty to animals. A walk with the dog should be a pleasant experience for both parties and not a violent tug-of-war. Here it is a question of getting the dog to submit itself to your will – that is, to get it to go where you want and at the pace you decide. But it is not necessary to teach the dog to march as if it was on parade, where it would lack freedom to move at all. It should be enough simply to teach it to walk nicely on the lead and stay on one particular side of you, and not weave from one side to the other. For certain strong-minded dogs simple teaching it to walk nicely is not enough, and therefore it is best to start training it early – firmly and with determination – as early as three or four months of age, and as soon as it has become used to a collar and lead. It is not very easy and can take time. Use a so-called choke-lead (it sounds worse than it is) or chaincollar and put it on your dog so that it can be pulled upwards. The lead should be 1½yd (1.3m)long.

Correctly placed chain collar

Incorrectly placed chain collar

1 Start with the dog on your left side. Here it is important to be quick with your praise. Do it as soon as the dog has taken the first steps without pulling on the lead. Continue to talk to it as you walk

2 Before long the dog will want to go its own way, and you must then correct it with a slight jerk of the lead. Use only the wrist, as illustrated. Too vigorous jerks can damage the dog's neck or back

3 Praise the dog and continue walking. There is no other method. Even a small dog must learn how to walk properly on the lead. You may be tempted to think that it is not necessary, that you can always 'manoeuvre' it with your little finger. Of course you can, but the dog can be hurt by struggling on the lead and eventually the throat, neck and back may be damaged.

Occasionally vary the exercise by making a right turn (it is the easiest) or a wide right-hand circuit. As soon as you deviate from the 'straight road', the dog will think that something interesting is happening and will want to follow you, forgetting to struggle

If you want to teach your dog the strict way of walking on the lead, that is, walking to heel, which can be a good thing if you walk in a town and which is a must in competitions, then you do as follows:

1 Choose an open place where you can be alone and where as little as possible can disturb the dog. At this stage work mainly with the lead and especially with your voice. The aim is to get the dog to walk at your left side with a slack lead. Keep the lead as shown in the picture and start by walking rapidly forward at the same time as you say 'Close'. In dog literature the word 'Heel' is often used, but I think it may sound a bit harsh, especially when the dog handler starts to become impatient (which he should never do).

Start by walking to the right. The dog will not then consider your body to be a threat but will think that the whole exercise is a form of 'follow my leader'

2 The whole training depends on your tempting and praising the dog. But if it becomes too interested in something else and starts to strain away in another direction or sits down on its hind legs and refuses to go any further, then you may have to correct it with some slight discomfort. Usually it is enough to use your voice: a short 'Close' followed by 'Good'. If the worst comes to the worst, you have to use a light, short jerk on the lead, at the same time as you say 'Close'. Repeat the word 'Close' when the dog is on its way back to your side and praise it with a pat and a 'Close, good' when it gets there.

Repeat again! Your praise should really give your dog a feeling of doing what is right and that the best thing it can possibly do is to walk by your side.

Do not continue training for too long. A few minutes at a time is sufficient. Let the dog rest between rounds and freely nose around. After all, training should be fun

3 If the dog is afraid, you could have problems with training it, and, if you correct it too harshly, you will only make the dog even more afraid. It is better that you ask somebody more experienced in dog training to help you. There are specially trained dog psychologists who can cure even the most problematic dog using scientific methods

4 The situation can also be just the reverse. Instead of the dog pulling at the lead, you can be the one who has to do the pulling in order to get the dog to go with you. This can only be because the dog is afraid, uninterested, lazy, in poor condition or not yet ready for training. Sometimes it can be difficult to decide what the reason is. Then it is even more important to tempt it with a friendly voice and a treat.

When walking on the lead is working well, you can supplement it with turns and swings. How this is done is shown on p80-1.

The final aim is to train the dog walking off the lead, when it can do the exercise without being attached to the lead (see p82-3) and becomes a confident and reliable dog which the handler can depend on – nothing could be better than a pleasant walk together.

RECALLING YOUR DOG

Dogs have a great need of exercise. They need to move freely as often as possible, but that means that they must be kept under control and be recallable at any time. The recall means that the dog must interrupt something it thinks is nice and that is why you must see to it that the reunion between you is even nicer.
If you know that your dog will come when called – and the dog knows it is always nice to return to you – then you have built the mutual trust which is the foundation for good social behaviour by the dog.

1 The recall is an exercise that can be varied ad infinitum and which must be practised all the time. It is important you can recall the dog at any time and in any situation – for instance, when it is sitting still, moving freely and even when it is together with other dogs

2 In most cases you and your dog are within sight of each other, but you should also be able to recall your dog when it cannot see you

3 At close distance you can recall your dog by calling 'Here' and maybe support the command by calling the dog by name. But you should also be able to recall the dog with, for example, a whistle which it has learnt to recognise

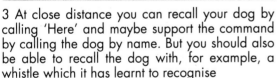

4 Do not forget that you must create such a relationship between you and your dog that it prefers being with you to anything else. That is why you must praise it properly and reward it with treats, playing with a ball or some kind of fighting game which the dog likes, when it comes to you under training. Never put it on the lead immediately after it has been recalled. If you do so, it associates being recalled with the restriction which this entails and which cannot be very pleasant. Recall training for the puppy is shown on the next spread

Recall training for the puppy

1 Walk the puppy on a fairly long lead

2 Catch its attention by calling 'Come' or 'Here' or any recall word you have chosen. At the same time give the dog a signal by pulling its lead lightly

3 As soon as the puppy starts to come towards you, back away in order to increase the distance between you, at the same time repeating the recall word you have chosen – for instance, 'Come' – once or twice with as inviting a voice as possible. You can also pull the lead lightly, if necessary.

Go on repeating 'Come', bending down or squatting so that your dog does not see you as a frightening giant. Lower your eyes too, so that the dog does not find them threatening. Pull the lead lightly if it hesitates.

Pat your puppy and praise it when it comes up to you. Give it a dog treat, too – it is supposed to think that coming to you is the nicest thing in the world

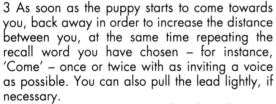

If you want to teach a more advanced recall for use in competitions, you can do the following:

1 When the puppy returns to you on call, guide it with the lead towards your right side, praising it warmly all the time

3 Sit your dog down facing straight ahead. Adjust its position, if necessary, all the same time praising it

2 Let it continue to walk around you and on to your left side at the same time as you change your hold of the lead

4 Add to the praise by giving it a dog treat and lots of patting. Again, teaching the pup something like this takes time and must be repeated again and again in order to get it right. Don't, however, let the puppy get bored with it. Remember to have lots of breaks for play in between, and also, spread the training sessions over a number of weeks

SIT!

The aim of the exercise is to get the dog either to sit facing straight forward at your left side or to sit down on the command 'Sit' wherever it happens to be at the time. 'Sit' is usually the first command that a puppy learns. Once the dog has learnt this, it is an excellent way of keeping control over it in all situations. Sitting is also the starting point for many obedience exercises. You can start this training at an early stage.

1 Place the dog on your left. Pull the lead straight up and push down the dog's back, at the same time commanding 'Sit'. Only a light pull is necessary. Ease the pressure on the dog's back as soon as you notice that it is starting to sit down. Do not place your hand too far back. The dog experiences pressure on the lower back as a sexual stimulus, which will have the opposite effect – the dog will resist the attempts to make it sit

2 If necessary, straighten up the dog and make it sit facing straight forward and praise it when it sits correctly. Remember that you must always be in command. If the dog tries to get up before you release it, you must repeat the word 'Sit' and push it down in the same way as before

3 The dog must learn to obey the command 'Sit' even from a distance, too. To make it easier for your dog to understand the command, you can support the command with a gesture – for instance, stretch out your hand at the same time as you say 'Sit'. Gradually the dog will learn to react to the gesture only (which must not be confused with the arm movement accompanying 'Down'), and you will not need to shout very loudly if there is a great distance between you

STAND!

Teaching a dog to get up on command might have no direct practical function but 'standing', meaning 'standing still', is an important part of the learning process and, in the same way as 'Sit', is a method of keeping the dog under control in all situations. To avoid a misunderstanding you could use the word 'Halt' as well, the main point being that you are consistent with the word you use. The necessity for consistency with the commands you use cannot be repeated enough. The world record for the number of commands that a dog understands is around seventy, so the 'vocabulary' of normal dogs is limited.

1 The aim is to get the dog to get up and stand still when you say 'Stand', and to remain standing until you order it to do something else. You can emphasise 'Stand' with a gesture

2 There are two ways of teaching the dog to stand from a lying position. Keep the dog on the lead and push the dog's groin lightly with your left hand, at the same time saying 'Stand'. Praise it as soon as it gets up

3 Certain dogs have very sensitive groins and, if this is evident, you could instead take hold of the lead near the collar and move your hand forwards and upwards at an angle, at the same time saying 'Stand' – that is usually enough

4 You might also stretch across the dog and get a grip under it with your left hand and, if necessary, help it up

5 After the dog has learnt this step, you may want to progress to practise standing at a distance. Start by standing fairly close to the dog while supervising it. If it tries to sit down, correct it with a short 'Bad', and if it shows signs of coming up to you, walk straight to it, place it back in the right position and start all over again

6 The next step is to teach your dog to stand still when you are out walking with it. Walk normally with the dog on the lead, then command 'Stand', continue walking a couple of steps yourself and then turn towards it. As usual, praise your dog generously

7 If this does not work and the dog comes towards you, you can do the following. While walking with it on the lead, first stop it with the lead, at the same time saying 'Stand', then walk a few more steps before turning towards it.

Then you can gradually progress to having the dog off the lead while commanding it to stand. Gradually increase the distance between you

DOWN!

The aim is to get the dog to lie down on command and to
remain there whatever might happen around it. If your puppy
is lively, this might be more difficult than it would seem.
You have to practise this exercise as early as possible
and repeat it often.
Gradually, as the dog obeys the command, you may increase
the time it stays down, go away while it is in the down
position and start the training with the dog standing
(as opposed to the usual sitting position) or even
moving around freely.

If you support the command with a clear gesture at the same time as you say 'Down', you will get your dog to lie down even if you are far apart. It is enough to catch the dog's attention with a familiar whistle, hold up your hand and bring it firmly forward and downward

2 Sit the puppy down and let it sit quietly for a while. Hold out a treat in front of its nose, but do not let it reach for it. Keep it back firmly with the lead

4 The puppy must lie down completely. If it does not, push it down carefully but firmly with your hand on its back

3 Bring your hand forward and downward, saying at the same time 'Down'. The puppy will learn to recognise the hand movement, which you must repeat each time you use the command

5 Reward your dog with a treat when it lies down properly, at the same time repeating the word 'Down'. Keep the puppy down by your hand signal (you do not have to touch it), and let it remain lying down for a short while before you let it get up. Preferably it should not get up until it receives the command

STAY!

It is often necessary to get your dog to stop immediately –
for example, it has no idea of traffic and, in an unguarded
moment, it may rush straight out among the cars –
maybe to say hello to an acquaintance across the
street or to investigate something interesting. The
aim of this exercise is to make your dog stand
(or sit) still until you come up to it and take over.
It must also be able to react to the word 'Stay'
only: it cannot see your visual signal when
it is going away from you.

1 In this exercise use both body language and
voice. When you raise your hand and say
'Stay', the dog must stop at once

2 The dog remains standing on the same spot until you walk up to it. In this exercise do not call the dog to come to you after 'Stay' but walk up to it yourself

3 The act of walking around your dog might not be necessary when you are out on your normal walk, but it is required for obedience tests

4 Not even the most well-trained dog can get enough praise and approval

TRAINING YOUR PUPPY TO STAY

1 Walk the puppy slowly on a fairly long lead

2 Stop, raise your right hand, giving a firm 'Stay' command. The puppy does not react at first but continues to nose around. When nothing happens, it finally stands still or sits down, usually turning towards you. Remain absolutely still all the while

3 Then, when the puppy is standing still and has seen your raised hand, gather up the lead and walk up it

4 Praise your dog and it will soon understand the connection between 'Stay', the signal, stopping and your approval

TURNING LEFT AND RIGHT

Remember that you are the leader of the pack, even if you do
not walk in front, and therefore it must always be you who
decides in which direction your dog should walk. Being
able to control your dog not only close to but also
from a distance, gives you a greater chance of being
able to let it move freely without it being on
the lead. That is something every dog
needs and enjoys, circumstances permitting.
If the teamwork between you functions
well, then this is a more efficient
method of control than using a lead.

1 Walk the puppy with a fairly long lead. Allow
it to go in front of you

2 Catch the dog's attention by calling its name,
adding the command word 'Right'

3 When the puppy has recognised its name and turned towards you, use body language and lean strongly towards the right, clearly pointing right with your arm

4 Follow through your turn to the right, at the same time pulling the puppy carefully to the right. Repeat the word 'Right' while following through the turn and praise the puppy as soon as it is heading in that direction

5 Teach the left turn in the same way, using the command word 'Left' instead

6 As usual, praise the puppy when it does well. Use exaggerated gestures to start with. Later you can 'semaphore' less. It might take time, but be patient

WALKING BY YOUR SIDE OFF THE LEAD

This exercise is rather difficult to teach and, before you start, your dog must be able both to walk at heel and to come when called. The command to be used is again 'Close'. Which method you choose for teaching walking off the lead depends entirely on your dog's individual character, but, having got this far, you know your dog well enough to be able to adapt the training to it. Some owners begin by walking their dog at their side while others start with the dog sitting next to them. In some cases it is best to treat this as a special exercise, while sometimes it is better to combine it with the 'Down' and recall exercises, etc. In other respects the training follows the normal pattern: correction when wrong and praise when all goes well. Variation is also necessary or the dog will get bored.

1 Have the dog walk, off the lead, on your left, its shoulder abreast of your knee. It must follow all your movements as if it was on a lead.

For most dogs, being unleashed means that they can move freely, but this exercise will teach them that it does not. If you are in control of your dog you may only have to use your voice to guide it. Start by gently removing the lead without the dog noticing. Give the command 'Close' and continue walking. Keep your hands in the same position as they were when the dog was on the lead

2 If your dog deviates from the 'Close' position, correct it with 'Bad' immediately followed by 'Close', and praise it as soon as it is back in position. In this way the exercise continues, sometimes for quite a while, since you must not resort to any harsher correction methods

3 You can also choose the two-lead method. Put two leads on the dog then take one off, making exaggerated gestures so that the dog really notices that you have released it. The dog cannot count and does not understand that you have another lead attached. Give the command 'Close' and continue walking. Use the other lead for correcting your dog's position if it leaves your side. Praise it when it is back in position

4 To make the dog associate any unpleasantness with actually leaving your side, rather than with you and the lead, see pp86-7, you can choose a third method. Use a fairly long lead which you keep short. Let the lead go and let the dog drag it along unaware, but hold your hands as if you are still holding the lead. As soon as it leaves your side stop the dog by treading on the lead. Repeat 'Close', and praise and reward the dog when it once more is walking correctly

WALKING IN FRONT

'Walking in front' is a term used mainly in connection with working dogs, as this is a skill which is needed for tracking and searching. It may not be very often that a family dog has to use such a skill, but it can be an advantage if the dog can walk on the lead some yards ahead when, for instance, it has to be walked on narrow tracks, across a foot-bridge or suchlike: this is what is meant by 'walking in front' and is quite difficult to teach. The dog does not feel the same 'pressure' from the handler when it walks some distance ahead of him, being much more curious about what is happening all around. You must therefore first have taught it the other stages of obedience before you start this one.

1 Start on a narrow path, preferably with high hedges on both sides, so that the dog is not easily tempted to stray. Keep it on the lead and move the right hand ahead, in a pointing gesture, at the same time as you say 'Forward'.

It is not easy for the dog to understand that it really is allowed to move 'freely' ahead of you – it has been trained to walk on your left side. Praise it therefore with 'Good dog' as soon as it moves ahead of you and repeat 'Forward'

2 It will take time, but gradually the dog will learn what the directing gesture means and will leave your side. Do not allow the dog to walk so far, however, that it starts to strain against the lead. If it does, check it with a gentle movement of the lead – an unpleasant jerk will only confuse it – and praise it again as soon as it walks correctly

3 You are the one to decide where you are going and therefore the dog must be fully aware of the speed you keep and where you are going. You must therefore keep contact with it all the time by chatting to it in a friendly manner (have you noticed how much the dog 'understands' when you are out walking alone with it and can tell it all about your worries?).

If the dog hesitates, you can direct it with the turning signals 'Right' or 'Left', which it has previously learned.

Long and patient training may be needed, but when the dog has learned how to walk ahead on a lead, you can start to teach it how to walk ahead without one

JUMP AND PLAY!

Even the most interested dog can sometimes get tired of
training exercises and will need to relax. Training is very
intensive and involves constant concentration on the trainer,
so the dog should be given regular breaks for relaxation,
and then be allowed to relax on its own terms: to rush
around, jump, bark, sniff and snoop, roll around in the
grass, dig in the ground or play with an object. A
high-spirited dog usually has no difficulty in occupying
itself. The only limit you should set is that it may not
play near heavy traffic, children or other handlers
and dogs occupied in some form of training.

1 When you reach a suitable stage in the training, bring the dog to your side. Talk soothingly to it for a while, and then unleash it and give it a cheerful, encouraging 'jump and play' signal

2 Make a 'be off with you' gesture, run a few steps yourself or throw a stick or a toy which the dog can fetch, without asking it to retrieve. Usually, it does not take much to trigger off the dog's propensity for play

3 Let the dog run around and play freely for a while, then call it. Do not put it on the lead immediately and do not restart the training straight away. Instead, squat beside it, praise it and chat with it for a while. It should be pleasant for the dog to come to you and it should not mean that the work, which is not always enjoyable, is about to start

GIVE!

It is amazing what a dog, and particularly a puppy, can take in its mouth and either chew or carry away – and at worst swallow. This is not only true outdoors, but your puppy can also in an unguarded moment indoors find things that are certainly not suitable to chew. 'Give!' is also a method of confirming the ranking order between you. If the dog learns it correctly, the command should enable you to take its favourite bone from its mouth without it protesting. Of course, you should not do this too often – it is possible that the dog will misunderstand your instruction and think that it should learn how to guard its 'property'. To start with, before the puppy has attained full confidence in you, it is a good idea to barter and give the puppy something in exchange.

1 Take a loose grip of the nose with the hand and press the lips of the dog carefully against its teeth, at the same time saying 'Give!'

2 If the dog does not let go, you can also take a grip with the other hand on the lower jaw, as illustrated, and pull carefully downwards. Praise and reward the dog as soon as it drops the object. Never try to pull the object. The dog will think that this is a game and it will keep an even tighter grip on it

If the dog swallows something dangerous

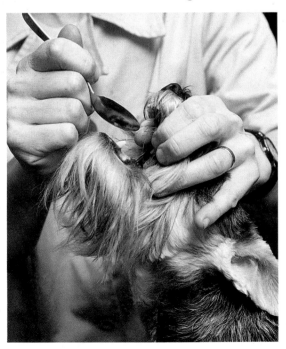

A healthy puppy can swallow the most remarkable things without ill effects, but if you notice that it has swallowed something which it cannot tolerate – you will notice this as it will snort and shake its head, cough and retch and generally look miserable – you must intervene immediately. It is best to get the dog to vomit up the object and the easiest way to do this is to open its jaws and put some rough salt, such as crystal salt, as far back on the root of the tongue as possible. It will be easier for the dog to get rid of the object if you lift it by its hind legs when it starts to vomit.

If the dog refuses to eat and vomits or retches in the morning before it has eaten anything, there is danger ahead. It has probably swallowed something that is causing a blockage in the intestines and you should take it immediately to the vet.

RETRIEVING

Could there be any possible use for making a dog run after an object that you yourself have thrown? It sounds like a doubtful proposition, but I know at least one circumstance when it is wonderful to have a dog that has learned to retrieve – when it has to be exercised in dreadful weather. Just imagine being able to stand under cover while the dog is kept intensely occupied for as long as you like. What makes it even better is that this exercise builds on a natural instinct so that the dog sees it as a game. It is relatively easy to teach a dog to retrieve, but it can be time-consuming since the dog must learn in stages. This exercise is based on playing, so you can start when the puppy is two to three months old, but you must not demand perfection. Before embarking on training, the dog must be able to do the recall (pp66-9), 'Sit!' (p70) and "Give!' (p88), because retrieving is nothing but a combination of all these exercises. The method might appear somewhat drawn-out and unnecessarily complicated, but the many steps must be co-ordinated, and this training is a good opportunity for owner and dog to get to know each other.

1 First, it is important to arouse the dog's inherent retrieving instinct. Start with waving a favourite object in front of its nose, but do not let it catch hold of it. When the dog is concentrating its full attention on it, throw the object a short distance. Wave your arm in a distinctive manner when you are about to throw the object

2 Run with the dog to the object, urging it all the time by commanding 'Fetch!'. As a rule, most dogs pick up the object straight away. If not, you have either thrown it too far away or not made it interesting enough. Start all over again.

Praise and reward your dog as soon as it picks up the object. It is natural if it does not want to let go of this hotly desired object, in which case use the word 'Give' (after all, it is yours)

3 Later, you can start using a special retrieving dummy. The dog will learn to recognise this quickly and know that it is for retrieving and nothing else. Then you can start demanding more, but before you do so, it is a good idea to prolong the playful part so that the dog does not get bored.

Start by putting the dog in the 'Sit' position at your side. Then you must stimulate the dog's desire to grab the dummy, but it must not do so until the command 'Fetch' is given. Let go of the dummy the moment the dog gets hold of it

4 Give the command 'Give' when the dog has had the dummy for a couple of seconds. Remember not to say it at the same time as you take hold of it. A lot of misunderstanding can spring from this. It is the 'Give' command that must get the dog to release the dummy, not your gripping it. Gradually increase the time between the 'Fetch' and 'Give' commands.

Dogs must bring back the retrieved object in pristine condition, so the next step is to teach your dog not to chew the dummy. At this stage most dog owners (and dogs) get bored and give up. You really need patience and stamina. Remember to be extremely liberal with praise and rewards. Any 'Bad' you say when you notice that the dog is showing an inclination to chew the dummy, must be followed immediately by praise and a pat the moment it stops

5 After this, let the dog walk with the dummy in its mouth. Say 'Fetch'. Let the dog pick up the dummy. Walk a couple of steps with the dog on your left, then stop. Say 'Give' and take hold of the dummy. Praise and reward the dog when it does so. That is all – apart from patience. Use the command 'Hold tight' occasionally when you walk. Increase the walks gradually

6 The next step is to train your dog to pick the retrieving dummy off the ground. There is a problem in that the dummy lies still and 'dead' on the ground and is not particularly attractive as an object for retrieving. Put the dog in the 'Sit' position and let it take the dummy from your hand on the 'Fetch' command. Repeat but hold the dummy closer to the ground each time. In the beginning you can wave the dummy to catch the dog's attention, but eventually it must pick it up from the ground. As mentioned previously, this lesson is not much fun for your dog (or yourself), so it is best to stop and do something else when the dot starts to get bored.

Teaching your dog to pick up the dummy is difficult. First, prop the dummy against a stone or a shoe, at the same time holding it with your right hand. Command 'Fetch', let the dummy go as soon as the dog has hold of it, and once more give the "Fetch" command.

The moment the dog has picked the dummy off the ground, say 'Give!'. If the dog does not pick up the dummy, you can make it more attractive by scraping it with your nail or wriggle your foot so that the toy moves a little

7 Practise, practise, practise, step by step! The next step is to get your dog to fetch the dummy. Keep the dog on the lead, throw the dummy a short distance away and, while it is still rolling on the ground, command 'Fetch'. Let the dog fetch it and then recall it. Say 'Bad' if it drops the dummy on the way back. Give the 'Fetch' command once more and, hopefully, the dog will pick it up again. If it does not, fetch the dummy yourself, let the dog take hold of it again and carry it back to the starting point. Do not forget to praise it after each part of the exercise is completed

JUMP!

In order that you and your dog are not hampered by obstacles when you walk in the woods and fields, it is a good idea to teach your dog to jump on command – and not to be too frightened to do so. After all, it is an advantage not to have to carry a dog weighing 50lb (23kg) or so across a ditch or a fallen tree. Jump training is not entirely without risk, and since a puppy's or a young dog's skeleton is delicate, you should not train it to jump until it is six months old. Take it easy in the beginning and make sure that the dog is warm enough before it starts the exercise. Let it gradually get used to higher obstacles. Note that some breeds should not jump at all.

1 Start with a very low obstacle – a few inches is enough, just high enough to make the dog aware of it. Put the dog in front of the obstacle and let it sniff an appetising dog treat

2 Take a few steps forward, at the same time saying 'Jump', encouraging the dog with the treat. If necessary, you can support the dog by carefully pulling the lead forward and diagonally upwards

3 Praise the dog and reward it with the treat as soon as it has jumped across the obstacle. Then increase the height in stages, but do not be in too much of a hurry. It takes time before paws and legs can tolerate long jumps. Also, do not make the training sessions too long

BALANCING

It is important for you to be able to take your dog everywhere in the woods and fields. Even the smallest dog can become very fit if it gets the right kind of exercise, and rough terrain is no problem with the right training. Dogs are not inclined to suffer from vertigo and are able to climb to considerable heights, but they are careful by nature and take no unnecessary risks. This exercise depends on mutual trust between you and your dog and it is not completely without risk – that is why practising it must be done calmly and carefully. If your dog is big it might be a good idea if, initially, you have an assistant to help catch it in case it falls. The dog should also be off the lead. If it hesitates, encourage it with a dog treat and push it lightly from behind.

1 Start on a low climbing frame. Most dog clubs have these at their training facilities. Coax your dog carefully, with the help of a dog treat, up the first rungs. Talk to it in a calm voice all the time

2. Continue across the horizontal part of the frame and try to keep the dog moving the whole time, or it might leap down to the ground from the top.

3 Bend forward and let the hand carrying the treat follow the slope of the ladder

4 Reward your dog when the exercise is done

FIND!

It is difficult to define how sensitive a dog's sense of smell is. It is said that a human being is 'smell-blind' in comparison with a dog. The cells in a dog's nose which enable it to smell occupy roughly the same surface as its whole body, while those of a human can only cover a small coin. Furthermore, a dog has a highly developed memory of smell. These are faculties for which we can have great use. The ability of mountain dogs to find people under snow a yard thick and the sniffer-dog's ability to detect very small amounts of narcotics are examples of this. Your dog, supposedly, will not have to engage in such serious work, but you could teach it to find mushrooms, for instance, or wild strawberries or the glove you lost.

1. Tie the dog with a fairly long lead to a tree at the edge of a large clearing. Take one of its favourite playthings – a chew or a ball is ideal – and play together intensively with it in order to arouse the dog's interest in the object.

2 Take the object and run zig-zag over the clearing. This means that the dog cannot follow the trail on the ground but must follow the scent left in the air by the object. Stop about 50yds (50m) from the dog, play demonstratively with the object so that the dog sees it clearly, and then place it on the ground, before returning to the dog

3 Unleash the dog and give the command 'Find', at the same time as you give it a gentle push in the right direction (you only need do this at the beginning). You may direct the dog by giving 'Go right' or 'Go left' signals with your arms.

When the dog finds the dummy, recall it. The perfect end of the exercise is the same as that for retrieving: the dog comes to you and gives you the dummy, and you reward it with praise and a treat

TRACKING

The ability to follow a trail is an art that in the best of worlds your dog will never need to practise. In a crisis, however, it is invaluable. A well-trained tracker dog can achieve miracles – for instance, it can find a child that has got lost in the woods. A dog that can track well is almost always right – if it indicates that the trail leads in a certain direction, you can be sure that the person you are looking for is there, no matter how impossible it looks.

1 When teaching your dog to track, work with a helper. Let him/her play intensively with the dog for some time, while you stand passively and watch

2 Put the lead on the dog, while your helper walks off a certain distance. Before moving out of sight, make sure that the dog sees the helper

3 Turn the dog around while the helper hides so that there is no chance of the dog seeing where he/she is

4 Now turn the dog in the right direction, point down at the trail left by your helper, and say 'Find'. When the dog finds your helper, the helper (not you) should reward it with a treat, while you may praise it

When you repeat the exercise, get your helper to walk off and hide in a different direction each time. The main thing is that the dog no longer can see the helper but must search along the scent trail without the help of its eyes

BARK!

Why should you teach your dog to bark when a whole section of this book has been used to teach you how to keep it quiet? If you sit alone in an isolated cottage or even in your flat in town and hear unfamiliar noises, it can be comforting if your dog lets you (and others) know that it is there and that it is alert to any possible dangers, such as intruders. It is not as difficult as you might think to teach it to bark. If you have a dog that is keen on barking, then you must first teach it to keep quiet on command, before you start to teach the command 'Bark'. It is, in fact, more difficult to get a dog that likes to bark to obey both commands, while a dog that normally does not bark very much can be taught to bark more easily. The commands used are 'Bark' and 'Quiet'.

1 Hold a treat in front of the dog's nose and say 'Bark'. Give it the treat as soon as it makes the slightest sound. Preferably keep it tied to a tree or similar object during the training, so that it does not jump up for the treat. If it does jump up for its treat, you will be forced to say 'Bad' and thus give double signals, which the dog cannot cope with

2 Repeat the exercise, but wait until the dog gives more definite sounds before it gets its treat. Continue the training and gradually prolong the waiting until the dog barks properly before you give it its treat. Repeat the word 'Bark' all the time. When the dog starts to bark, you should encourage it continuously until you give the command 'Quiet'. You may emphasise the command by holding your hand in front of its nose

CRAWL!

Crawling is not a natural movement for a dog, so that it is difficult for it to learn. What is the object of teaching your dog to crawl? If you have taught it to track and search, being able to crawl forward in restricted places can be an advantage. Sometimes it might help if you want to move through difficult country. Remember that crawling is very strenuous, so do not let your dog crawl for long stretches, even when it is fully trained. Regular breaks are important.

1 Start by making the dog lie down on the command 'Down'. After it has placed itself in the correct 'Down' position, wait for a couple of seconds. Then with one hand hold a treat in front of its nose and move it slowly forward, while with the other hand press the dog's back lightly, saying 'Crawl' (the waiting time prevents the dog from connecting the two commands and forming the habit of starting to crawl as soon as it is 'Down')

2 Crawling is not a natural way of moving for a dog, so reward it liberally for moving even a couple of inches. Then increase the distance gradually. It helps if you have it on the lead and to pull it gently forward and downward once it starts to move. It is important that the ground is soft – preferably a lawn – and that there is nothing in the vicinity that will disturb the dog

3 You can also teach your dog to crawl by placing it on one side of a low bench. Put its lead under the bench and go around to the other side. Pull the lead lightly and say 'Crawl'. Praise the dog and reward it as soon as it has reached your side

4 The next stage is to teach the dog to continue crawling after it has passed the obstacle. Do this by holding a treat in front of it, repeating the word "Crawl" if it shows any inclination to get up. Be prepared to push the dog down on the ground with your other hand, if it continues to try to get up, but let go as soon as it really does lies down properly.

When the dog is properly trained you can order it, even from a distance, to get down and crawl

PACK AND DRAUGHT DOGS

Most dogs like to show how strong they are, so getting them to carry loads or to pull a child on a sleigh or cart is usually not difficult. The difficulty is to train them to do it in an organised manner.

It goes without saying that not every breed adapts to this training and under no circumstances should the dog be overworked. Dogs with a short, strong back, such as riesenschnauzers, are especially suitable for carrying a pack. Spitzes, alsatians and rottweilers make particularly good draught animals. The dog must be at least two years of age, sturdily built, and in good condition. The height of the withers must not be less than 20in (50cm). At this stage, it has learned to walk 'Close' and to come on command. Use only specially made packs, harnesses and shafts of the best quality. If the equipment is faulty, it can do considerable damage to the dog.

WALKING WITH A PACK
1 First, let the dog get used to the pack. Put it on empty in the beginning. Distract the dog if it tries to get rid of the pack by scratching and biting it

2 Practise recalling the dog and bringing it to heel when it is wearing the pack. Never put a pack on a dog that you do not know or do not have control over

3 When the dog is accustomed to the pack, you can start loading it, stage by stage. Loading instructions usually come with the packs when you buy them. Take care that the pack is smooth and comfortable where it touches the dog. Sharp objects should be placed towards the outer side of the pack. A well-trained dog can carry up to a third of its weight.

Train the dog by going for short walks in varied terrain

A DRAUGHT DOG

1 The teaching procedure is the same as for walking with a pack. First let the dog get used to the harness. Keep it on the lead on the first few occasions when it pulls the sleigh or cart.

Practise recalling the dog and bringing it to heel, with the sleigh or cart empty, and then gradually increase the load. A well-trained dog can pull a load of 60–80lb (27-36kg). Start with short distances and increase them gradually. Never let the dog pull a load in difficult terrain because it can easily become stuck and, also, the risk of an accident is great

2 Always keep the dog on the lead if you let it pull children.

CYCLING

The bicycle is an excellent tool for exercising, both for the dog and its owner, but it must not be used to extremes. It could become too monotonous and the dog can easily become exhausted. The surface on which it runs – particularly rough gravel and asphalt – can badly wear both pads and legs. There is always a certain risk involved in cycling with a dog, so you should not do it in town traffic. Also, the dog perspires by panting and thus inhales considerable amounts of exhaust fumes if it runs in a town. Do not start the training until the dog can walk to heel and come when you call it. Wait until the dog is one year old before you start to cycle with it.

1 First let the dog get used to the bicycle. Keep the dog on the lead and put the bicycle between it and the traffic

2 Mount the bicycle and kick yourself forward, feet on the ground, so that you can stop immediately. Stretch out your arm with the lead so that the dog is not too close. Correct it with a slight tug outwards if it still gets too close

3 Stop immediately and say 'Bad' if the dog tries to jump up at you. Praise it if it runs correctly by the side of the bicycle, but speak quietly so that it does not become excited and think that it is a game

4 Mount and start to pedal. Talk reassuringly and cycle with only the free hand on the handlebars. If you must use both hands, hold the lead so that the dog cannot pull you off the bicycle if it suddenly decides to run off

TAKING CARE OF YOUR DOG

HEALTH CARE

Daily check-up

To ensure that your puppy feels as well as possible, you should make it a habit from the start to do a daily health check-up. It is a matter of a simple routine, which can mean a lot to your dog's health and development.

If your puppy, which is usually very playful, suddenly becomes listless you should ask yourself the following questions: is it only tired; does it not feel well; has it broken a claw and got an infection; has it chewed and swallowed half a shoe; has it got toothache; or has something else happened? It can show that something is wrong, but it cannot tell you what it is or how it feels. With regular check-ups of the following kind you can quickly find out if something is not in order, and then you can do something about it in time.

Coat Comb and brush the puppy's coat. If it is long-haired, check that the coat is not tangled. If you notice that the puppy often scratches itself, this can be due to lice or fleas, in which case you should consult a vet. But it can also have been in contact with some substance to which it is sensitive (the coat was possibly badly rinsed when the dog last had a bath, or it splashed around in dirty water when you went out last time). If this is the case you should rinse the coat very carefully again. If the dog still does not stop scratching, you should see a vet.

Check also to see if your dog has ticks. There is a method of getting rid of them, but the risk of infection is great. If they obviously do not bother the dog, let them fall off by themselves.

See also Grooming, p117.

It is not just physical care that your dog needs every day

Teeth The puppy's teeth must be cleaned at least once a week. Use a normal toothbrush and dip it in lightly salted water. Remains of food at the base of the teeth can easily cause infection, and you should also use a toothpick between the teeth. Chewing-bones and marrow-bones are also excellent means of keeping the dog's teeth clean.

Check that the milk teeth loosen when the second teeth start to appear. If double teeth form it is usually easy to loosen and pull out the milk tooth.

Many dogs get tartar which must be removed by a vet. It gives the teeth a brown-yellow colour and the breath an evil smell. You can clear a mild attack of tartar yourself if you buy a special tartar-scraper.

It does not matter if the puppy breaks a milk tooth, but a broken second tooth must be taken care of by the vet.

Ears A dog's ears are very sensitive. The ears of long-haired dogs are particularly difficult to keep clean, so you should pull out the hair that is situated at the innermost part of the auditory canal, or have it done at a trimming clinic. Luckily, it does not hurt as much as you might think, as long as you do it gently and take small amounts at a time. Wash carefully inside the ears with a damp face-cloth.

If the dog starts to scratch its ears frequently and shake its head, you should consult the vet. Do not try to clean the ears yourself by poking them with a cotton ear-bud or similar utensil. Often this only makes the problem worse.

Eyes Use a clean damp cloth to wipe away any dirt that may have gathered in the corners of the eyes. Never poke around the eyes with your fingers. Eye discharge of any kind is a symptom that there is something seriously wrong with the eyes and you should consult a vet as soon as possible.

Paws You should ensure that the pads are undamaged and soft. You must treat them with a special salve if they dry up and/or start to crack. Cut the claws regularly. How you do this is shown on pp121-22. Cut the hair between the pads and check at the same

Big or small, all dogs need daily love and care

time that there is no fungoid growth on the skin patches.

Weight You do not need to weigh the puppy every day, but there are weight curves for the growth of most breeds, and you should check occasionally that your puppy more or less follows them. If your dog is overweight, it can cause wear on both legs and paws, and if it is too thin, it will lose its resistance to diseases. In both cases, the dog's health will deteriorate. A dog readily eats all the food it is given and it is therefore necessary that you check the menu carefully.

Miscellaneous Bitches can often get cancer of the teats. You must therefore examine them regularly to see whether any lumps have formed. At the slightest suspicion, take her to the vet.

Male dogs often get an infection of the foreskin. It is irritating for them but usually harmless and is cured easily by washing with a disinfectant.

113

THE DOG BATH

How often should you give your dog a bath? Very young puppies should not have a bath at all. They have such a woolly undercoat that it is difficult to get them completely dry, which makes them vulnerable to infections. The coat contains natural fat which protects it from water and dirt, so a bath will do more harm than good.

For fully grown dogs the rule is simple. Give them a bath whenever it is necessary. Do it at night after the dog has been out – it should not go out after a bath until it is completely dry. On the whole, dogs like having a bath but, if they are frightened early on, they can turn a session in the bathroom into a water polo match. So take it easy at the beginning and let the dog decide the tempo.

1 Never let the dog jump into the bath-tub by itself – or out of it for that matter – however eager it is for a bath, because it could easily slip and hurt itself. Once a dog is frightened, it is difficult to get it back into the bath. Lift it instead – even if it is big and heavy – and talk to it to make it relax. Put a rubber shower mat or a rough towel in the bath to prevent the dog from slipping

2 Shower the coat thoroughly. The water should be about 86°F (30°C). Do not open the taps too much because the noise and splashing can frighten the dog. Start from underneath and work forward – bottom, hind paws, stomach, front paws and chest. Keep the dog's head up and away from the shower so that it does not get water on its face or in its ears. Most dogs will accept having cottonwool put in their ears when they have a bath, which is very good protection. Then work your way over the back, keeping the head clear of the water all the time

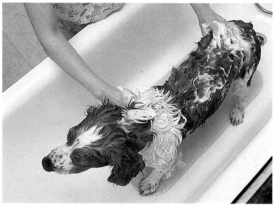

3 Wash the coat with dog shampoo, doing the head last. Take care not to get shampoo in the dog's eyes. Then rinse very carefully, from the head backwards. If the dog is really dirty, you might need to repeat the procedure

4 Leave the dog in the bath-tub for a while. It will, without fail, shake off the water and it is certainly better for you if it does it there. The amount of water contained in a dog's coat is incredible!

5 Wrap a towel around the dog and lift it up. Drying a long-haired dog is a big job, so if you can put it on a table, so much the better. Squeeze the water out of the coat along the lie of the hair, using a couple of towels. Then use a hair-drier, checking first that the air is not too warm. However, be very careful when you first introduce the dog to the hair-drier, as the noise and the sensation may frighten it

OUTDOOR SWIMMING

Many dogs love water – you just cannot stop them when they want to jump in. But the fact is that dogs should not go swimming because of the dangers of infection. At public beaches the water is supposed to be clean enough for swimming, but quite properly dogs are not allowed there, and if you go anywhere else, you have no way of knowing if the water is polluted or not. Of course, if you have access to a private beach or there is a secluded spot where you swim yourself, then you can take your dog along for a swim.

Never force a dog into the water if it does not want to go, and do not encourage it to jump in the water from jetties and rocks. Water will certainly get into its ears and this can cause inflammation.

If your dog insists on having a swim, the same rules apply to both of you – do not swim too far away from the beach and do not go into the water immediately after a meal.

Whatever happens, you should give the dog a shower as soon as you are home, especially after a swim in salt water.

Do not swim too far out and leave your puppy alone on the beach. If it sees you disappearing into the unknown and does not dare to go in itself, it may well panic and you should not let it suffer in this way.

All dogs know how to swim but it is difficult for the long-haired breeds to swim long distances. If your dog should get into difficulty and almost drown, the instructions on pp58-9 show how to revive it.

GROOMING

The condition of your dog's coat has a direct effect on the condition of its skin. A dog that is not groomed will be attacked by skin problems sooner or later and then the vicious circle sets in: if a dog has skin problems, it will develop a coat without lustre which may even flake in patches.

Through planned breeding, breeds have been produced with many types of fur – short, smooth and long, coarse and woolly, and even hairless dogs. The breeding process has also influenced the skin – for example, bulldogs, bloodhounds and bassets all have skins that are several sizes too big!

There is a large range of grooming accessories which have been specially adapted for each breed. Most good pet shops can help you to make the right choice.

It is important to get the puppy used to being groomed as early as possible. Work on a firm table that is not too big, as a wobbly table will make the puppy feel insecure and it will want to get down. Put a rubber mat (you can use the dog's shower mat) on the table to give the dog a firm base. Get used to lifting the dog onto and off the table – even when it is fully grown. Remember that you are the pack leader even in this situation, so if the dog resists or tries to jump down, you must correct it by saying 'Bad' and continue to work on the coat. Speak to it calmly and praise it when it stands still. It is important to 'table train' it so that it is not unduly worried by a visit to the vet, for example.

Start by untangling any knots in the coat. Particularly sensitive areas are the stomach and recesses such as behind the ears, under the tail and the groins. Start by trying to pull out the knots with your fingers. If the knots are very difficult – which they should not be if you go through the coat every day – you could, as a last resort, cut them off. But cut lengthwise, as a barber does, and never across, which would leave ugly marks in the fur. There are special creams for use when the dog has a bath which makes knots easier to untangle.

If you have a breed with an oversize skin,

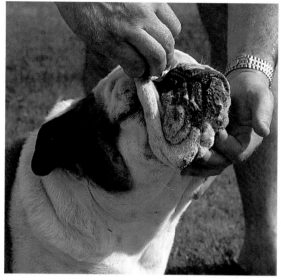

Or should we call it 'beauty care'?

you must pay particular attention to the folds. They must be cleaned every day or bacteria will gather there which may cause inflammation and other problems. The same applies to the wrinkles around squat noses and the corners of the mouth on dogs with pendulous lips.

Certain breeds have pendulous eyelids and streaming eyes which may cause ugly marks on the fur, and the eyes must therefore be wiped at times. Small applications of a special cream can help to prevent the marks.

Brush short-haired dogs with a medium to stiff brush. If you want the fur to gleam – and who does not? – you can polish it with a piece of chamois leather.

Long-haired dogs and dogs with thick furs – for example, spitzes – need to have their coat carded before combing.

Comb most dogs in the direction in which the hair lies, but breeds with bushy fur should first be combed along the lie of the hair and then roughly against it.

Each breed is trimmed in a special way to correspond to a fixed beauty standard. It is best therefore to leave your dog's beauty care to a specialist. There are at least as many hair fashions for dogs as for humans, even if the fashion does not change as quickly. As it takes a hairdresser five to six years to become fully trained – and he/she cuts only the hair on customers' heads – you can understand that dogs' hairdressing is not to be attempted without a thorough knowledge of the subject.

The following illustrations show basic trimming which you can do yourself but if, for instance, you want to show your dog, you should leave the grooming to an expert. However, ask if you can be present when your dog is groomed and you will learn more and more. Most trimmers are generous with their good advice. There is also special literature which deals with cutting and trimming.

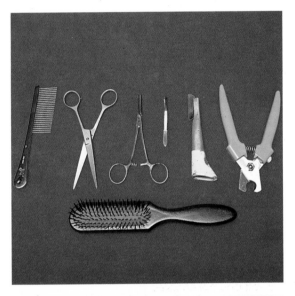

Grooming equipment
This is the basic equipment that is necessary for keeping your dog's coat and skin in prime condition. From the left:

1 Comb
2 Scissors
3 Surgical scissors
4 Tweezers
5 Stripping comb or dresser
6 Nail clippers
7 (*Below*) Carder

1 Always lift the dog onto and off the table. Sometimes it must also be made to lie down. This is a dominating action and practice is necessary. When the dog understands who is in charge it will remain lying down, which makes the work much easier

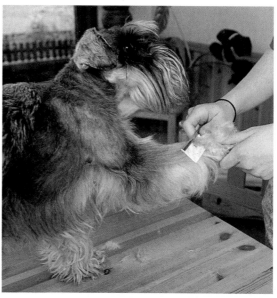

2 Brush or card all tangles and mats in the coat. At the same time check if the dog has any parasites, such as ticks. Make sure that you go all the way through the coat to the undercoat. Be firm but gentle

3 Comb the coat with a special comb. Work calmly and methodically and talk to the dog all the time. Hold it in a firm grip – a dog's fur is not sensitive like our hair is, but the dog may jerk if it hurts, and sometimes kick wildly if it gets bored with the procedure

4 Trim around the paws. This is especially important if there is snow on the ground, since icy lumps form easily if the hair on the paws is too long, which makes walking difficult

5 Cut the hair between the pads. If it gets too long it annoys the dog when it is walking, and it also amasses a lot of dirt. Check that the pads are soft and not cracked

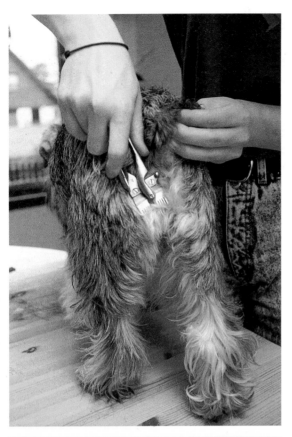

6 Trim around the ano-genital area. This is important for hygiene. There are special scissors for this job, but you can also use ordinary blunt-ended scissors

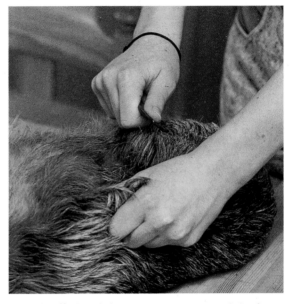

7 Pull off dead hair using a special knife. It sounds frightening, but the dog feels nothing if you are careful. It stimulates new hair growth

8 Trim unnecessarily long hair in the ears. It is very important that long-eared dogs' ears are 'aired' and kept clean properly to reduce the risk of infection. You can use ordinary blunt-ended scissors. Keep the dog's head in a gentle but firm grip so that it does not suddenly toss its head

TRIMMING THE NAILS

It is very important that you trim your dog's nails at regular intervals. This is especially true for small light dogs whose nails easily grow too long. Also, if the dog lives in a town and walks mainly on asphalted or paved streets, its nails will not wear normally and you must be twice as careful.
Nails that are too long do not just make walking difficult for the dog, they also break easily, and this can be extremely painful. They might cause the dog to tread incorrectly.

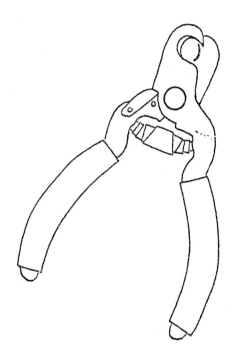

NAIL

NAIL BED

WRONG!

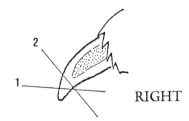

RIGHT

1 Never use scissors or any other form of pliers, but buy special nail-clippers and a nail-file in a pet shop. The nail bed, the soft inside of the nail, is very sensitive so that it must be cut carefully and correctly. If you are hesitant to cut your dog's nails, you might ask somebody at a dog-trim parlour to show you how to do it. If the dog has light-coloured nails, it is easy to see the outline of the nail bed and from this you can see how much to cut. Content yourself with trimming the nail tips if you are at all uncertain

 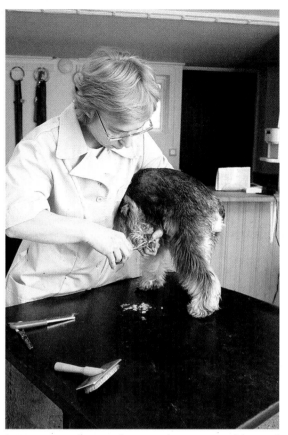

2 If you have a small dog you can hold it as shown when you cut its nails. If you hold it firmly and talk to it quietly and in a friendly manner, it will, as a rule, keep calm and not wriggle too much. But it is important that it should not feel captive. If you notice that it is becoming worried or irritated, it is better to interrupt the trimming and start again after a while

3 You can place a bigger dog on a table and press it lightly against you as shown. If you then carefully lift up one leg at a time – like shoeing a horse – there is usually no problem.

Do not forget to check the dew claws, if your dog still has them. If the dew claws get too long, they may hook into each other and cause the dog unnecessary suffering.

In most breeds the dew claws should be removed in puppyhood

Ce qu'il y a de meilleur dans l'homme, c'est le chien.

'The best thing about a man is his dog'

T-N Charlet (1792–1845),
French artist

Love, affection, trust, protection, company and joy – the list
of what a dog can give you is long. This book has concerned
itself mainly with what you can teach your dog, but I am
sure that you will discover, when you have lived with your
dog for some time, how much it can teach you.

INDEX